237
INTIMATE
QUESTIONS
...Every Woman Should Ask A Man

LAURA CORN

Park Avenue Publishers

Browse our Website

www.grrreatsex.com

237 Intimate Questions
. . .Every Woman Should Ask A Man
By Laura Corn

Published by Park Avenue Publishers
fax (310) 452-1323
phone (602) 829-0131
P.O. Box 1453A 14th street, Suite 116
Santa Monica, CA 90404

Website address: grrreatsex.com

Library of Congress Cataloging in Publication Data
Corn, Laura
TX-0-9629629-1-3

1. Sex Instruction. 2. Sex. 3. Man-woman relationships.

ISBN: 0-962-9628-8-0

10 9 8 7 6 5 4 3 2

Book Design by McMan & Tate-Los Angeles
mcmantate@earthlink.net

QUICK START GUIDE

● There are lots of different ways to use this book. You can either ask the questions in numerical order, by icon, or in whatever order you want to. I guarantee you'll turn him on!

● When you see an icon below the question, that means you'll find men's uncensored, outrageous answers to that very same question sealed up in the back of the book. No peeking! (---not until you ask *your* guy first!)

● Each question is paired with a quote from one of 82 best-selling sex and relationship books. You can either read the quote silently to yourself, or aloud to your partner, before you ask the question. (Totally cool and informative)

● The Laura Corn Challenge starts at question 207. There you'll begin to quiz your guy on all matters sexual. These 31 trivia questions have real answers. (Also sealed up in the back!) And again, *remember* --- no peeking until he takes the quiz!

● Atmosphere is important! That's why I've come up with some really grrreat settings for each icon. (See next page)

● Try not to ask too many questions in one sitting. Always leave 'em wanting more!

●Timing is everything. Ask him the questions when you've got his full attention, not when he's trying to watch the game or stressed out after work.

● Remember: There are no right or wrong answers--until you get to Laura Corn's Challange, that is. The key is to be attentive and totally nonjudgmental.

● Most importantly, the goal is to have fun. So keep a smile in your voice and a sparkle in your eye, and have a wild, okay wonderful time!

THE ULTIMATE LEGEND

= Sunday Afternoon Delight! Ask these on the couch while giving him your best hot-oil foot massage, and he'll be putty in your hands!

= Auto Erotica! Whether you're going on a road trip, parking on Lover's Lane, or driving to the movies, these fun questions are guaranteed to keep his motor running!

= Party of Two. These questions would be fun to ask in a dimly-lit restaurant--corner table, candlelight, bottle of wine, loooooong tablecloth. You won't make it to dessert!

= The Great Outdoors. Ask these questions outside--on a stroll, in your yard, or walking down the beach. Afterwards, he'll want to beat around *your* bush!

= The Ultimate Foreplay. Pose these questions while eating breakfast in bed on a weekend morning. Do it before you make love and you'll be in a state of exquisite expectation!

= Saturday Night Fever. These questions are best asked on a Saturday night in your favorite room of the house. Surround yourselves with tons of pillows and candles, and wear your best lingerie. He'll really want to light your fire!

= Weekend Getaway. Pose these questions at an amazing hotel, in a bubbling Jacuzzi, or in a faraway city, and he'll feel like he's been given a Passport to Pleasure!

= Potluck! Ask 'em anytime, anyplace, anywhere--as long as you do it when he's least expecting it. He'll be hanging on to your every word!

= Wild Card! These questions are scattered throughout the book. You never know when one might pop up... just like a guy!

= Laura Corn's Sexy Sex Quiz. I double-dare you to ask these questions at a bar or party with a few of your closest friends. (If you chicken out, pose them while lounging on your living room floor.) Be sure to keep score, and your man will be hoping to score by evening's end!

No Icon = You can ask these questions that don't have icons anytime, either with the questions in each section, or just follow your whims. You won't find answers for these in the back of the book...but there are no wrong answers, so ask away! He'll be begging for more!

V

ACKNOWLEDGEMENTS

I am deeply indebted to:

Jeff Petersen – Without your support, I would never have been able to write all these books about romance, relationships, and Grrreat Sex. And without your love, I wouldn't have even wanted to. You taught me what it was all about, Punkin.

Marty Bishop – As always, your words and your wisdom have infused these pages with a special light. You have made me a better writer.

Julie Taylor – You are the closest thing to a miracle I have seen this year! I can hardly believe how fortunate I was to find you, at exactly the time when this project needed your skills and insights. (A special note to readers: Julie is a very successful free-lance writer. Currently, her first screenplay is being made into a movie, and her articles are frequently featured in Cosmopolitan, and other national magazines.) This book would not be possible without you.

Michelle Fox – my assistant, and now my friend and confidant. Also one of the coolest people I know! If I could have invented a sister, she would have been just like you. Did you ever think the simple act of putting words on paper could be so hard? Your boundless energy made this book possible. Your advice made it better.

Meg Gallagher – My oldest friend, and mother of my godchild. You've done some great things in your life, Meg, but Grace is your crowning achievement.

Bill Wright - Who took a chance on me when no one else would. Bill, you launched my career, and I am eternally grateful.

Much & House Public Relations - Especially Sharon House and her assistant Kelly. You guys are everything a PR firm is supposed to be. (And I'm only sorry I didn't find you so much sooner!)

Login Consortium - The whole crew, especially David Wilke and Susan Shaw. You're the best at best-sellers! Here is hoping for many more to come.

Bill Bricker - Who created the whole stylish, contemporary look of this book, front to back. Bill, I wish I could have used all of the great designs you showed me. You're a genius! Not to mention how much fun you are to work with. I'm so glad I found you.

Michael Carr - Who took my words from a bunch of rather messy computer files and turned them into these beautiful pages.

A Special Thanks to: Scott Kelly, Susan Sullivan, Michelle Faulkner, Lorraine Daye. And every one at PMA – especially Joyce.

Thank you Morning Mouth, Bit Board, Don Anthony & Allison, Radio Star, and all the other terrific radio prep services who keep telling their subscribers to put me on their shows. And to the men and women of RADIO – Appearing on your shows is my very, very, very favorite part of this job!

Special thanks to those of you who took part in my survey, and whose words appear in the sealed pages at the back of this book. And finally, my thanks to you . . . and everyone else who has purchased my books through the years. I would love to hear about your experience with these questions! You can tell me all about it at www.grrreatsex.com.

Introduction

Ladies, what's the one little thing that can instantly make your relationship more exciting, sexy, and fun? A few hints: It doesn't cost any money, but it will make you both feel like a million bucks. There's no sex involved, but you'll feel like you're having grrreat sex. It has the power to make you serious one minute, then have you laughing your butt off the next. It takes little effort, but can instantly change your relationship overnight. What is this secret cure-all, you ask? And where can you get it? Right here! Yep, this magic relationship-booster is simply...

A question.

That's right--a question. And you've got 237 of 'em right in your hot little hands. All guaranteed to turn him on, crack him up, make him think, and shock him speechless. How do I know? Because over the past 9 years, I've asked over 1,000 guys these very same questions in person or on the airwaves. Some laughed, some cried, some ranted, some raved. Heck, a few even fell in love with me sight unseen! But every single man I talked to absolutely fell head over heels for the experience. Why? Because there's nothing more exciting than someone who's genuinely interested in you. And these questions make a man feel good. And when a man feels good, he's gonna open up. And once he opens up, you'll never believe what you'll find!

You know how everybody says that guys don't like to talk about their feelings? Well, they're obviously not asking the right questions! I swear, every guy I spoke with practically talked my ear off! This is because each of these 237 questions was designed with the boy brain in mind. You know how guys are way more visual than verbal? Well, I've written tons of visual questions to really get them going. And the question sequence is specifically designed to make sure he never gets bored. You might spend 20 minutes on one question and 30 seconds on the next. Some will send him walking down memory lane. Others will have you laughing so hard, you'll have tears running down your face. And more than one will make you want to rip each other's clothes off so badly, you might have trouble even getting to the next question! And that's okay. Because this is a book you can pick up wherever and whenever you feel like it and easily pick up where you left off. A book you can pull out at parties and instantly be the center of attention. A book that guarantees you'll never again be at a loss for words.

These seriously sexy questions have the power to literally change your life, and make him fall in love with you all over again. I truly believe the quality of your life is determined by the quality of questions you ask. Just think about the success of Oprah Winfrey, Barbara Walters, and Jay Leno. If they asked boring questions or didn't prepare for their interviews, do you think millions of people would tune in? No way! When Letterman has someone in his hot seat, he doesn't just stare at the person and wait for them to say something interesting, does he? Nope—he asks questions that will provoke interesting answers. And this book will help you do the same thing!

Not that I'm saying you have to plan and prepare for every conversation with your partner, mind you. If you've read my Grrreat Sex books, you already know I'm a big fan of spontaneity. But I also believe that great conversations--and great sex, for that matter—doesn't always just happen. Sometimes we need a little nudge. And that's what these questions will give you: a push toward better conversations, deeper intimacy, and—most importantly—lots and lots more fun!

*I*t's a blast learning so many unexpected nuggets of info about your man, and you can use that knowledge in virtually every area of your relationship. After I asked my sweetie, Jeff, the 237 questions, I designed a whole romantic adventure based on the things I'd learned. I pitched a tent on the beach, because he'd told me he loved camping. I packed it full of red pillows since he'd revealed that, to him, red was the color of passion. And I had a cooler full of the goodies he'd told me he loved nibbling on right after sex. I had absolutely no clue about any of this before—but now that I did, I was going to use it! So when your guy says something zany, file it in your Mental Rolodex and pull it out when he's least expecting it. Like Jeff, I'm sure he'll be totally blown away!

*B*efore you get started on your own adventure, you only need to know two things: How to ask and How to listen. "Duh!," you're probably thinking. "I already know how to do that!" Of course you do. But for these questions to elicit the amazing, incredible responses that your guy is totally capable of giving, the way you ask and the amount you listen are critical. You've got to ask him these questions in a non judgmental way. Have fun with it! Put a smile on your face and in your voice. Look him in the eyes, then let your gaze wander to his lips once in a while. Let him know you think he's the Stud of the Earth. And listen, listen, listen. Ladies, how many good listeners have you met in your lifetime? Probably not many, eh? Most people don't listen, they just wait for their chance to talk! But this time, really hear what he's saying. If he tries to ask you the question, go with it—then put the focus back on him. If you do, he'll tell you things you never thought you'd hear coming out of his mouth! You're not gonna believe it!

*A*nd when should you ask these wild and wonderful questions? Since most people tend to zone out after working all day, I don't recommend asking them during the week. There are exceptions, of course, but the key is to talk when you can really talk. Not when the kids are wailing in the background or Monday Night Football's on or when you're surfing the 'net. This has to be your only focus. And, once you get started, I guarantee it will keep your attention. Boy, will it ever!

*W*here you should ask the questions is another story. Obviously anywhere is fine, but certain questions simply beg for an amazing setting. I've designated those with a special icon—a high heel, diamond, moon, star, chili pepper, or daisy. The Ultimate Legend box in the beginning of the book tells you where you should ask those spectacular questions—so run, don't walk, to check it out! And these nifty symbols also mean those questions have answers in the corresponding sealed envelope in the back. Yes, sealed—whoo hoo! There, you'll find all the outrageous, uncensored answers I've compiled from my 1,000 amazing interviews. Most of these you totally have to see to believe! But remember: No peeking, no matter how bad you want to! The questions are so much more exciting to ask if you don't know the other guys' answers beforehand. And you'll notice that not all of the questions have an icon. That's because they're new, and I'm still compiling answers for my next edition. Please stay tuned!

When you see the "Light Bulb" icon, it's time to play "The Laura Corn Challenge," my own one-of-a-kind trivia game. The rules are simple: You ask your guy a number of tantalizing trivia questions—like what the number-one sexual fetish in America is, or what "crawling the wall" means. And guess what? Unlike the other questions, these actually have right-or-wrong answers. You'll find the correct answers sealed up in back, so...no peeking until you ask your guy the questions! Since the questions are pretty off-the-wall and unbelievable, I don't think even Dr. Ruth could get them all right! But if he gets 20 of the 31 right-he wins an amazing back massage. 25 correct? Surprise—he gets a personal strip tease, performed by beautiful you. And for 31 right—he'll receive your love-slave services for an entire evening! (And you better call the Guinness Book of World Records, because they'd probably love to know you're with the World's Greatest Sexpert!)

As you ask these positively provocative questions, your guy will be wild with passion, intoxicated by your interest, and drunk with desire. He'll be fascinated with you because you'll be fascinated with him. After all, we all crave total attention and unconditional love. That's why the brain is the greatest sex organ in the body. As I always say: "When you turn on the top head, the bottom one will follow!"

I'm so excited that you're about to embark on this journey. Even though I had a ball asking guys all across America these 237 questions, I never had more fun than when I asked my own guy each one. Discovering his intricacies and quirks made me love him all the more, and our bond grew that much stronger. And we had the most fun we'd ever, ever had. I learned things about him that I wouldn't have guessed in a million years! I just know the same thing will happen to you. When your question and his answer meet, it's like your souls are kissing. And there's absolutely nothing in the world more awesome than that!

Wishing you a lifetime of great questions, great answers and all the happiness in the world.

Laura Corn
Santa Monica, California
January 2000

X

1

START HERE

"I don't mind living in a man's world, as long as I can be a woman in it."

Marilyn Monroe

Q: What makes a woman unforgettable?

2

TURN ONS
Lonnie Barbach

*S*hort, tall, big, small – bodies are wonderful in their infinite variety. Exposing your body and playing it as a fine instrument to arouse your partner can add exciting fun to your lovemaking. Creating an exotic striptease is a great way to do this.

Get dressed in something sexy. Turn the music up and the lights down. Gather a few scarves and pretend you're on the stage of a personal strip show. Seat your partner comfortably in a chair or on the bed.

Get into the mood by dancing seductively to the music. As you slowly remove your clothing—item by item—keep your eyes riveted on your partner. Drape the scarves across your semi-clothed body and brush sensuously against your partner. Throw your inhibitions to the wind—this is the time for seductive play. Both men and women can do fabulous strip-teases once they get into the mood.

Q: If a woman did a slow, soft, sensuous strip tease for you and left just two things on, what would they be?

3

LOVE NOTES FOR LOVERS
Larry James

*I*ntentionally add a little pizzazz to your love relationship every day. Do it in a playful way. Exercise your sense of humor. It enlivens your spirit, breeds happiness, and causes you and the one you love to experience fully the love you feel for one another. Do things that make each other smile. Smiles and knowing nods from your lover create a sense of unity that adds longevity to your relationship.

Q: If you could pick the one thing that always makes you smile, what would it be?

4

SECRETS OF THE SEXUALLY IRRESISTIBLE WOMAN
Graham Masterton

*P*utting nipple clamps on a stranger means very little, even if that stranger happens to be your partner. But doing the same thing with somebody whose feelings and needs you really care for...that's what makes it really exciting. Marla, for instance, a twenty-seven-year-old art student from Los Altos, California, said, "I love being dominant, and whatever you say about it, men don't mind at all. In fact they love it. You couldn't say that my current boyfriend, Raymond, isn't a real man, but nothing turns him on so much as having me spank his bare behind with my hairbrush—yes, the bristly side. Then I hold his penis very tight, digging my fingernails in, and give his pubic hair a good stiff brushing!"

Maria is a good example of the sexually irresistible woman. She makes sure that she gives her man everything he wants...even some of those variations that he fantasizes about but has never plucked up the courage to suggest.

Q: What's the most unusual item you've used during lovemaking that really turned you on and rocked your world?

5

IN THE MOOD

Doreen Virtue, Ph.D.

Date Night

*E*very couple needs to date, regardless of how long they've been together. Just like an exercise program, which takes effort and planning but which yields tremendous benefits, a weekly date ensures that your love will stay healthy and vital.

If you take only one step toward improving your love life, this must be it. I've discovered, when working with couples like Terry and Wendy, that both partners are anxious to have a fun, happy relationship. Neither partner wants a routine, overly-responsible life that is devoid of great sex or passionate romance. Usually, however, both partners feel that the other person should do something to improve the situation.

Since both partners feel overwhelmed by their day-to-day responsibilities, they resent the "obligation" to create romance in the relationship. "Don't I do enough already?" is the angry thought accompanying this dilemma. So, they wait for their partner to pull a romantic trick out of his or her hat.

Q: If you had to take one action today to improve your love life, what would it be?

6

SECRETS OF SEDUCTION
Brenda Venus

*W*ho you are as a man is who you are in bed. That's why life and sex flow into each other. To get, you have to give, and that includes passion. To please a lady you must be willing to go out on a limb. If you're afraid to take a risk, you'll miss all the fire a woman has to offer. So, let your heart and spirit soar!

Women love men who have confidence. Nothing is more sexually exciting than a man with a feeling of certainty about himself; a man who knows how to move, how to dress, how and when to touch a woman. I'm not talking about 'macho' or 'cocky' - that's *pretending* to be a man. I mean the kind of man whose assuredness springs from the depths of his soul. He's genuinely positive; he doesn't pose or assume a phony attitude. He's as real as a tiger!

Q: If you had to name the one thing you wear that makes you look sexy, what would it be?

7

THE GUIDE TO GETTING IT ON
Paul Joannides

*I*s getting tattooed a sexual thing? Who knows. It sure is popular these days, especially among women who are sporting little butterflies, flowers and the like in highly private places.

Piercing, like tattooing, has been around for a long, long time. Women have traditionally had their ears pierced, as have various pirates and sailors who have sailed the seven seas. Nowadays everybody seems to be getting into the act, although the recent male ear piercing craze appears to be slowing.

In a highly sexualized version of piercing, body parts like noses, navels, nipples and genitals are potential sites. People who are seriously into piercing will stick earrings or gold posts through just about anything. Some do it for sport, others experience it to be on the sacred side with body as altar.

Some people say that getting nipples pierced hurts more than having genitals done, others disagree. One woman who sports gold rings along the sides of her labia says that the jewelry dresses up her genitals and makes her like them even more. Another woman who has had her clitoris pierced loves the new sensations and claims that just sitting down can sometimes give her an orgasm.

Ah, life in the big city.

Q: What's the most erotic tattoo or body piercing you've ever seen? Would you like to see that same look on your lover?

8

THE 7 SECRETS OF REALLY GREAT SEX
Graham Masterton

air, makeup, and jewelry come under the heading of "dressing to thrill" too. If you've had the same hairstyle since leaving high school, maybe it's time you went to your hairdresser for something more startling. Change your color or change your cut. I talked to literally scores of men about what clothes and hairstyles they found the sexiest, and over 60 percent said they were aroused by very short spiky crops or short hair slicked back with gel. Thirty percent said that they liked long blonde hair, but the impression created by girls with very long hair or elaborate hairstyles was that they were more interested in their own appearance than they were in giving a man a good time. Dan, from Madison, Wisconsin, told me, "I once went out with a very pretty girl whose blonde hair was so long she could sit on it. But it was like going out with two people instead of one—her and her hair. It was always 'Watch my hair!' or 'Your watch strap's caught in my hair' or ' I can't go out tonight...it's raining and my hair will get wet.'"

Q: *"Blondes have more fun!"* Or do they? What's the difference between blondes, brunettes, and redheads? Of all the women in the world—*other than your lover*—whose hair would you most like to touch?

9

HOT SEX
Tracey Cox

"*My* girlfriend puts a hell of an effort into our sex life. Each time we have sex, she'll introduce something new — whether it's a position, a technique, or a location. It used to freak me out. I couldn't help obsessing that she'd done all this with someone else (or was doing it on the side and picking up tricks that way). Then I figured she just had a vivid imagination and was really into sex. She drives me nuts outside the bedroom, but there's no way I'm letting go of her."
   - Neil

Q: Since the thrill of the chase is so exciting, how can she keep you hot on her trail—even after she's already been caught?

10

HOT SEX
Tracey Cox

*O*pposites don't attract, similarity does. Couples who have the same values, attitudes, interests, and ways of looking at the world are more likely to say they've found "a soulmate" and more likely to stay together. On the other hand, hooking up with someone whose differences complement your own personality is a good idea. That's why worrier-relaxed and shy-outgoing combos work.

Q: Opposites attract–or do they? Thinking about all the people closest to you, what are your most striking similarities and differences?

11

THE 7 SECRETS OF REALLY GREAT SEX

Graham Masterton

*E*ven if you're not dressing specifically to be sexy, it's always worth taking extra trouble with your clothes and your appearance. It's a compliment to your partner, a way of showing him that you think he's the best. Don't overdo it, however. It's possible to wear too much in the way of facial cosmetics while trying for a look of absolute perfection—hair, teeth, nails, trim figure, etc.—whereas some of the sexiest women are the women who look well groomed but accessible. Nothing deters a man more than a woman in a power suit with claw-like nails, highly polished shoes and a flawless coiffure that's a masterpiece in solidified hair spray.

Q: If a woman was only allowed to wear two types of makeup for the rest of her life, which ones would you choose? And what's the one cosmetic you'd most like to ban for life?

12

REAL AGE
Michael Roizen, M.D.

*S*urveys show that the average sexually active American has sex about once a week (fifty-eight times a year, to be precise), although there is clearly a variation. Married people tend to have more sex than single people. Frequency also varies over age, economic, and social and ethnic boundaries. One of the first studies to track aging longitudinally, done at Duke University beginning in the 1950s, found that the frequency of sexual intercourse (for men) and the enjoyment of sex (for women) correlated with longevity. In other words, people who had sex more often lived longer. Other studies found that sexual satisfaction became a predictor of the onset of cardiovascular disease: Both men and women who were less satisfied with their sex lives were more likely to have premature aging of the arteries.

Q: Do you think the quality or quantity of sex is more important? Why?

13

SECRETS OF THE SEXUALLY IRRESISTIBLE WOMAN

Graham Masterton

*W*ear clothes that show your confidence in yourself. Avoid the overweight woman's uniform of bright Hawaiian colors, elastic waistbands, and billowing tops. Dark, subdued colors will flatter you much more and give men the impression that you take yourself seriously. A low neckline under a tailored suit always looks good—provocative but businesslike, both at once. Avoid stretch pants or leggings at any price. Although they're comfortable, they show every single bulge and lump, and they're desperately unflattering, even on thin women. Buy blouses and tops and skirts that fit you, even if you wince at the sizes you have to buy. For the fuller-figured woman, the key to looking sexy is to look smart. There is nothing more off-putting than that "I know I'm fat so I've let myself go to seed" look.

Q: Congratulations - you're now a member of the fashion police! What's the first thing that should be outlawed on women in public? What should be a felony at home?

14

THE ART OF KISSING
William Cane

*K*issing should stand alone as a sensual pleasure that deserves to be enjoyed for itself without going on to other sex acts. Kissing can bring two people closer than —— because it's a more personal interaction. Which is why many prostitutes won't kiss their customers. They'll —— for hours but won't kiss, because kissing is considered even more intimate than ——.

Q: What's your favorite type of kiss?

15

MORE WAYS TO DRIVE YOUR MAN WILD IN BED

Graham Masterton

I want a friend, I want a wife, I want a lover, I want a whore, I want a princess, I want a critic, I want a business partner, I want a hostess, I want a mother for my children; I want someone who makes me laugh, someone who understands me when I'm down, someone who forgives me when I'm unjust, and stands up to me when I'm angry. I want someone who can walk into a room beside me and make me feel like I'm royalty. I want someone who can talk dirty and really turn me on. I want someone whose lips can speak words of warmth, words of reason, and words of judgment, yet will use those same lips to kiss my penis.

Q: If you were to pick the one alluring quality that draws you to a woman and keeps you there, what would it be?

16

HOT MONOGAMY
Dr. Patricia Love and Jo Robinson

*P*eople project much more positive images when they put conscious effort into their appearances. When the color of your clothes flatters your coloring, when your clothes fit well, when your clothes are well cared for, you make a strong first impression. It doesn't matter if you are old or young, tall or short, fat or thin, plain-looking or beautiful. The effort you put into looking good says, "I care about me. I'm worth the effort." When this attitude is reflected in your posture and the way you walk, the effect can be stunning. People are drawn to you. They think you must lead an interesting, full life. They want to spend time with you.

You were given only one body. Whatever its present size or shape, it's the only body you have. Dress it up and take it out! When you look as good as you possibly can, you will feel better about yourself, which will ultimately make you feel more sexually alive.

Q: What makes a lady a *lady*—and what makes her look like anything but?

17

203 WAYS TO DRIVE A MAN WILD IN BED
Olivia St. Claire

*A*fter getting the okay from him, truss him up. Use silk scarves, his own necktie, soft ropes, your stockings, or anything else soft but strong enough to hold him. Fasten him, spread-eagled, to the bedposts, or simply tie his feet together and hands behind his head or back. Then tease him. Let him inhale your highly personal aroma. Caress and kiss him everywhere but his genitals. Brush your nipples and your pubic hair over his stomach, chest, and up to his mouth, but make him wait awhile before allowing him to lick you there. Take advantage of his helplessness by tonguing his underarms – a very sensuous undertaking that should leave him panting. Masturbate him. Suck his frantic penis. Play with him like a favorite toy. And then, at last, get on top of him, slip him inside, and thrust fast and passionately. Untie him right away as his post-orgasmic muscles will quickly get stiff. To put the icing on the cake, you might even massage the cramps out of his muscles and soothe him into a relaxed glow.

 If she was going to show you who's boss in the bedroom, what mini-dominatrix moves would have you begging for more?

18

BEING A WOMAN
Dr. Toni Grant

*T*his is it: the ultimate female fantasy of being "taken," trans-ported, ravished, "swept away" carried over the threshold of love in the arms of a valiant hero. It is a theme of countless books and movies, perhaps the most popular of which is that spectacular scene in *Gone With The Wind* where Rhett carries Scarlet up the stairs. The sight of the gargantuan brute King Kong scooping up delicate little Fay Wray in his huge hairy paw is another great cinematic vision of ravishment.

Surrender. The very word conjures of visions of defeat, of shame, of submission. Yet in love, as opposed to war, surrender is sweet, for it enables the woman to fulfill her deepest feminine potentialities, both sexually and emotionally.

Q: She's 100% woman. But what percentage of your lover's personality is: Good Girl, Bad Girl, Angel, Bitch, and Everything-in-Between?

19

EMOTIONAL INTELLIGENCE
Daniel Goleman

*A*n early warning signal that a marriage is in danger, Gottman finds, is harsh criticism. In a healthy marriage husband and wife feel free to voice a complaint. But too often in the heat of anger complaints are expressed in a destructive fashion, as an attack on the spouse's character. For example, Pamela and her husband, Tom, went to a bookstore. They agreed to meet in front of the post office in an hour, and then go to a matinee. Pamela was prompt, but there was no sign of Tom. "Where is he? The movie starts in ten minutes," Pamela complained to her daughter. "If there's a way for your father to screw something up, he will."

When Tom showed up ten minutes later, happy about having run into a friend and apologizing for being late, Pamela lashed out with sarcasm: "That's okay — it gave us a chance to discuss your amazing ability to screw up every single plan we make. You're so thoughtless and self-centered!"

Pamela's complaint is more than that: it is a character assassination, a critique of the person, not the deed.

Consider this finding: Even after thirty-five or more years of marriage, there is a basic distinction between husbands and wives in how they regard emotional encounters.   Women, on average, do not mind plunging into the unpleasantness of a marital squabble nearly so much as do the men in their lives.   The conclusion, reached in a study by Robert Levenson at the University of California at Berkeley, is based on the testimony of 151 couples, all in long-lasting marriages.   Levenson found that husbands uniformly found it unpleasant, even aversive, to become upset during a marital disagreement, while their wives did not mind it much.

Q: What type of woman turns you off emotionally and sexually? Is there a difference?

20

SECRETS OF SIZZLIN' SEX
Cricket Richmond & Ginny Valletti

*W*hen viewing your nakedness in the mirror and negativity pops up...don't get hysterical! Wink, smile, seductively shrug your shoulders and affirm: "Who can resist lovable me?" Stand tall, strut, pose or stretch and belt out, "Baby, you got it." Blow extra kisses to scars, wrinkles, veins or other less-than-perfect areas. Accept them as trials and recorded history of where you've been. Use the mirror to watch yourself dance or prance till it feels good and looks inviting. Giggle, laugh, sing and rejoice at being the heavenly love goddess you are. Remember, keep repeating positive affirmations until they become a part of you.

Q: When does a woman's body look the most beautiful to you?

21

THE GUIDE TO GETTING IT ON
Paul Joannides

*F*or some men, putting their fingers between a woman's legs is a moment that has its own wonder or magic. They love feeling the woman's warmth and the start of her wetness, and how her body sometimes tenses, squirms and writhes. The arc that jumps back and forth from fingers to thighs is sometimes quite intense.

Q: What do you think about when you touch a woman's inner thigh?

22

THE GUIDE TO GETTING IT ON
Paul Joannides

*W*hile most vaginas feel quite nice, some feel even better. And once or twice in a lifetime a man might encounter a vagina that feels so amazingly wonderful that the mere memory of it redefines his personal concept of heaven. Interestingly, one never knows how a particular vagina is going to feel based upon the appearance of the female to whose body it belongs. For instance, steam might be billowing out of your ears at the mere sight of a certain woman, but after having intercourse with her your penis complains that jerking off in the shower feels better. At the same time, a woman who seems quite plain on the surface may be the one whose vagina you remember most throughout life.

Q: You adore your lover's hot little kitty. But what is your absolute favorite thing about it?

23

HOT SEX
Tracey Cox

"When I was about 13, I put a finger inside me while lying in bed and waited for the fireworks to go off. Not surprisingly, nothing happened. I actually didn't have an orgasm until I was about 22 when I found my roommate's vibrator. Over the next year of so, I experimented with it: moved it in a circular motion, teased myself, tried different pressure. But the problem with vibrators is that you don't really discover how to give yourself pleasure because the machine does it for you. After I moved out, I deliberately didn't buy one and taught myself to masturbate with my fingers. It took a while, but now I can orgasm within about five minutes."

- Jennifer

Q: Which do you find more erotic: a woman who masturbates with her fingers or a woman who masturbates with a toy?

24

HOW TO BE A GREAT LOVER
Lou Paget

*O*ne man, a lawyer from Boston, told me that what gets him most excited is when his wife (a history professor) puts on his boxer shorts and tank top. "When she's wearing that outfit, I go crazy!" In fact, I have it on very good authority that when women wear jeans and a T-shirt it is every bit as much a turn-on for some men as a garter belt and push-up bra. I've even known men who simply cannot resist a woman in soft flannel pajamas. Above all else, you need to be comfortable with your presentation. Your comfort, both in mind and body, is the key to your sexual freedom.

Q: If a woman had to wear the same clothes for an entire week—frequently washed, of course!—what would you like to see her wear?

25

SECRETS OF WORLD CLASS LOVERS
Jaid Barrymore

*T*hen again, one of the most stimulating enhancements to lovemaking of all time is, of course, music. I once read a quote that said, "If music be the food of love, play on." I couldn't agree more. From the thunderous crescendos of Tchaikovsky's "Love Theme" from *Romeo and Juliet* to Rachmaninoff's *Piano Concerto No. 2 in D Minor* to Richard Wagner's beautifully romantic "Liebestod" from *Tristan und Isolde,* all of these pieces have inspired my lover and me to the most passionate lovemaking we've ever experienced.

Sometimes our taste is totally different, however, and what we're in the mood for is raw, hot rock'n'roll music..

Q: What's the best CD to play during sex?

26

THE 7 SECRETS OF REALLY GREAT SEX
Graham Masterton

*T*here is nothing at all degrading about your partner wanting to see you dressed in erotic underwear. Quite the opposite, in fact. He is paying a compliment to your sexuality by showing you that you are just as exciting to look at as a Playboy centerfold and that you can more than compete with other women when it comes to turning him on. Remember that men are extremely visual in their sexual responses.

Many men find it very difficult to ask their wives or girlfriends to dress up in sexy clothing, mostly because they fear the embarrassment of refusal, or the old "What kind of woman do you think I am?" response. That's why they tend to spring erotic underwear on their partners as unexpected gifts—and quite often it's the unexpectedness of it as much as the gift itself that causes the woman to react in a negative way, and leads to arguments, misunderstandings, and resentment.

Q: How would you turn a good girl *bad*?

27

SINGLE WILD SEXY AND SAFE
Graham Masterton

*P*erhaps the most famous use of visual stimuli was Sharon Stone's quick flaunting of her pantielessness in the movie *Basic Instinct.* I'm not suggesting for a moment that you walk around with no panties, opening your legs to every sexy man you meet, but you can use this and other visual teasers to keep your own man's sexual interest at a very high pitch.

The "no panties" trick is one of the best. Actually, you don't even have to show your beau that you're not wearing any panties. All you have to do is whisper to him, halfway through the evening, "I forget to put on my panties." Then see what effect it has on him. Nobody else will be able to see whether you're wearing any panties or not, but your man will stick to you like Crazy Glue for the rest of the evening-just in case-and believe me, he won't be able to think about anything else.

Q: What sexy celebrity do you most feel women could learn from?

28

WOMEN ON TOP
Nancy Friday

*T*he most popular theme of male fantasy also reverses reality. How burdensome and tiresome it is for men to always have to make the first move, be responsible, in charge, and how understandable that they should wish to flee from all this hard work and imagine women happily taking on all the sexual initiation, giving the men no choice but to lie back and *be done to* for a change.

It is equally burdensome and tiresome for some women to play passive little girl. It requires a great deal of effort and not much happiness if the role doesn't fit. Some women have always had the IN CHARGE fantasy and repressed knowledge of it. No longer.

Q: Would you like your lady to pursue you sexually more often? What percent of the time would you like her to make the sexual advances?

29

THE LOVERS' BEDSIDE COMPANION
Gregory J.P. Godek

A gentle touch; a simple gesture; a kind word; a wink of an eye; a simple gift; a big surprise; a little surprise; a dinner out; an evening alone; a hot bubble bath; a moonlit stroll; a walk on the beach; a day in the park; a night at the opera; a secret message; a special song. The expressions are myriad, the meaning is one: "I love you."

Q: When you're in love, what's the one thing that you can't get enough of?

30

HOW TO HAVE MULTIPLE
ORGASMS
Janalee Beck

$\mathcal{K}$issing is a unique, special mode of communication. A definite turn-on. If a man hasn't kissed you on the neck, shoulders, forehead, breasts, butt, toes, armpit, back, earlobe, or behind the knees—you haven't really been kissed adequately. (Minimally, he should choose seven out of ten places) And let's not forget to return the favor!

$Q:$ Quick! What are your lover's top seven moan zones?.

31

HOW TO BE A GREAT LOVER
Lou Paget

*T*he Perfect Place for a Hand Job.

One of the many advantages of a hand job is that it can be done in a variety of places. Intercourse and fellatio (forgive me ladies, "blow job" just isn't my favorite term), even excessive kissing, are difficult to overlook when being done in public. However, a good hand job can practically be done under the nose of a stranger without detection. It's been known to happen in such places as in restaurants (providing the tablecloth is long enough), in airplanes (those little blankets are good for something), and on amusement park rides (though you may have to go around more than once). Although admittedly, the risk involved is part of the thrill, by all means, do be careful. Being arrested is another serious mood killer. Basically, men are thrilled by a good hand job outside of their bedrooms.

Consider these reported favorite locations:
- Stairwells of hotels, libraries, or office buildings
- Boardroom tables
- The boss's desk (who knew this was so popular!)
- A restaurant powder room
- Laundry rooms
- Under the beach blanket
- The kitchen counter, when on your way out of the house for the evening

 Your lover has just tied your hands behind your back and wants you to tell her how to give you the ultimate hand-job. What tips and tricks do you give her? And where's the wildest place you've ever received manual stimulation?

32

THE SENSUOUS WOMAN
By "J"

*M*ore men than you would believe thrive on a slight sense of danger. Men pick amazing places for sexual adventures. Some of the more trustworthy gentlemen I interviewed acknowledged that they had intercourse in -- are you ready for these? -- the Tomb of the Unknown Soldier, New York's Philharmonic Hall the week it opened, the ladies room of the Harvard Club, the choir loft of a church (I heard several variations on that one), underneath the bleachers at a rodeo, a band shell in a park on a rainy day and a department store window (the shades were closed) at night while the window was being decorated. The male animal seems to thrive on such nuttiness.

Q: Where are the best places to have a quickie besides the bedroom? And what's the most amazing quickie you've ever had?

33

MEN, WOMEN AND RELATIONSHIPS
John Gray, Ph.D.

*E*very day, a woman needs to receive some form of verbal reassurance that she is loved. This means saying things like, "I love you, I love you, I love you, I love you, I love you, I love you, I love you, I love you... ". There is basically one way to say it and it needs to be said over and over.

Men sometimes stop saying "I love you" because they want to be new and original. They imagine that a woman would grow tired of it or become bored by it. But saying "I love you" is never redundant. Saying it is actually a process of allowing her to "feel" his love. He may love her, but if he doesn't say it, she won't feel it.

Q: If you love someone, how often should you tell them?

34

REAL MOMENTS FOR LOVERS
Barbara De Angelis, Ph.D.

*H*ave you been putting your lover on a "verbal love diet" without realizing it? Are you doling out little tastes of love that leave your lover hungry and always wanting more? Or perhaps it's your lover who's been starving you by controlling the amount of love words he gives you.

Most of us need to learn to use more words of love, and not fewer words. And most of us need more verbal love from our partners. Words of love will feed your partner's heart and nourish her spirit. How many more of our relationships would survive and flourish if only we were more generous with our words!

Q: If you had to name the one thing ever said to you by a lover that you wish you could hear again, what would it be?

35

THE GUIDE TO GETTING IT ON
Paul Joannides

*R*omance In Long Term Relationships – Getting The Mix Right

When it comes to long term relationships all the romantic gestures in the world are meaningless if you aren't trustworthy and don't help maintain the mutual nest. Cooking a special dinner or sending an unexpected card won't get you far if you didn't do any of the chores that your partner was counting on you to do.

For romance to work in a long term relationship, it needs to be based on a foundation of reliability and trustworthiness. Then, the kind and thoughtful gestures that we are calling romance have a footing on which to stand. They help take your relationship beyond the functional and into the sublime.

On the other hand, when you hear people who have been together for a long time say that the sparkle is gone in their relationship they have sometimes worked so hard on being reliable that they have forgotten about the little gestures that help to make a relationship fun.

Q: What are the major factors in a lasting relationship?

36

5 MINUTES TO ORGASM
D. Claire Hutchins

A majority of women who masturbate do so within four minutes, a statistic that is almost identical to men's. Why then are we so much slower at reaching orgasm during intercourse?

Q: Is lovemaking measured in time, or orgasms? Is it always better if it lasts longer, or does the length of a bedroom session have no effect on the amount of pleasure you receive?

37

THE TEN-SECOND KISS
Ellen Kreidman, Ph.D.

*T*here is no question that touching sustains life. Research indicates that receiving hugs significantly increases the supply of oxygen to all the organs in our bodies. Even a simple touch can reduce the heart rate and lower the blood pressure. Touch also stimulates the release of endorphins, the body's natural pain suppressers. The healing touch of massage boosts immune function, improves the ability to concentrate, lowers anxiety, and has been shown to have positive effects on colic, hyperactivity, diabetes, and migraines. Instinctively, we've known for ages that touch is life-enhancing. When Michelangelo painted God extending a hand toward Adam on the ceiling of the Sistine Chapel, he chose touch to depict the gift of life.

Q: If you had to choose between a hug or a kiss, which one would you choose and why?

38

SECRETS OF WORLD CLASS LOVERS
Jaid Barrymore

*W*hile we're on the subject of cinematic smoldering, another way to participate in your favorite scenes from your favorite films with your lover is by renting them and watching them at home in the privacy of your cozy living room or your inviting bedroom.

You can either watch each film you like in its entirety, or you can become really creative, if you allow yourselves the time and patience. Just make a list of your favorite sexy films, rent them at your video store and tape just the "good parts" back-to-back on the same tape. You know which ones. The ones you anxiously await while the rest of the plot seems almost like filler, until you get to those too-hot-to-handle scenes that drive you so crazy that you lick your chops wishing it were you on that screen.

Q: What movie would you have loved to have been the leading man? And what starring role would be perfect for your lover?

39

GOOD VIBRATIONS GUIDE TO SEX

Cathy Winks and Anne Semans

*P*lease allow us to set the record straight: A dildo is not a penis substitute any more than riding a bike is a substitute for taking a stroll. A dildo is an object which allows you to penetrate yourself or your partner in a marvelous variety of ways. Dildos are a logical, dare we say, natural response to the fact that while many of us enjoy having our vaginas or anuses filled, no two of us have exactly the same preferences in terms of the length, width and shape of the object filling us. Why should your experiences with penetrations be defined by the dimensions of your current partners' penises or fingers? Few of us limit our dining experiences to eating only whatever is in the refrigerator at home. Think of dildos as the takeout food of the sexual realm; they offer novelty, spice up your routine and teach you about the range of your appetites.

Q: You're starting a website called "SizzlingSex.Com." On it, you recommend that every couple in America have certain passion props in their little bag of tricks. What are they?

40

DAVE BARRY'S COMPLETE GUIDE TO GUYS
Dave Barry

*P*robably the fastest-growing sector of the U.S. economy is the sector that conducts surveys asking women what is wrong with men. About every two days you read yet another newspaper article stating that 92.7 percent of American women find men to be pathetically inadequate in some ways. What two major areas of male deficiency are revealed by these articles?

- Housework
- Orgasms

Why Men and Women Have Trouble Getting Along:

At the risk of generalizing, I would say that the basic problem can be summarized as follows:

WHAT WOMEN WANT: To be loved, to be listened to, to be desired, to be respected, to be needed, to be trusted, and sometimes, just to be held.

WHAT MEN WANT: Tickets for the World Series.

Q: What do you think a woman needs to be truly fulfilled? And what does a man need?

41

HOT SEX
Tracey Cox

"*Why* does she hate it if I look at porn mags? Do I give up now on her ever watching porn with me?"

Ever since Hugh Hefner launched Playboy in 1954, women the world over have gotten their panties in a wad over pictures of women not wearing any. The fact is, the majority of men don't watch porn for the sinister reasons women think they do. They do it because it's fun. Most men are turned-on by main stream porn (which doesn't include material involving children, animals, or extreme violence). Because men are better at separating love from sex than women are, they consider porn films an innocent "boy thing," and most can't understand why girl friends take offense. Quite frankly, neither can I if we're talking about the old copy of Playboy or Penthouse or an occasional X-rated video. Just don't expect her to watch or read it with you unless she wants to—and if she's extremely anti-porn, yes, give up now on ever sharing it with her.

Q: What adult video do you think every woman should watch at least once, and why?

42

HOW TO MAKE LOVE ALL NIGHT (AND DRIVE A WOMAN WILD)
Barbara Keesling, Ph.D.

I tell men: Embrace your penis! Put out the welcome mat. Open a dialogue. Let it know it's a part of you and let it know you care. It's time to bring your penis in from the cold. The sooner you do, the sooner your sexuality will start to change. Now here's the best news. If you like your penis, your partner is going to like your penis. If you're proud of your penis, your partner is going to be proud of your penis. If you embrace your penis, your partner is going to embrace your penis. Sound Good? I thought it would.

Q: I think it's fair to say that men have two heads. Which *head* do you follow?

43

LIGHT HIS FIRE
Ellen Kreidman

*S*ince most men aren't accustomed to hearing compliments about their bodies, they don't know what they're missing. Believe me when I tell you that the first time a woman tells him what gorgeous sexy eyes he has, or compliments him on his strong legs, he's gone! Although they are unaware of it, most men are starving for this kind of attention.

Notice Your Man
· Notice his muscular legs
· Notice his masculine chest
· Notice his handsome face
· Notice his gorgeous head of hair
· Notice his sexy eyes
· Notice his beautiful smile
· Notice his broad shoulders
· Notice his large, masculine hands
· Notice his deep voice
· Notice anything that makes him a male

Q: For just a moment, put aside all thoughts of modesty. What one feature do you get the most compliments on? What's your most sensual feature?

44

SECRETS OF SIZZLIN' SEX
Cricket Richmond & Ginny Valletti

*W*hether Dolly-dimensioned or luscious little love bumps, all breasts are fully loaded with sensory nerves that can be instantly activated. Size in no way symbolizes sexiness, touch sensitivity or reaction satisfaction. Although some females climax solely from breast arousal, most of us need additional nudging below the belt. Perhaps more women would take heart and hug those honeys if given some entertaining encouragement.

Rubbing nipples with Ben-Gay or similar heat-producing creams will warm more than your heart. Don't however, use analgesic products on genitals. Better yet, purchase user-friendly Hot Stuff body oils and lavish them abundantly on bosoms. Feel your temperature rising as you lift mams to your mouth and gently blow. No oil available? Simply moisten a finger with saliva or sexy secretion and apply...hummmmmmm.

Q: Besides your sweetheart, who's got the most beautiful breasts you've ever seen?

45

DRIVE YOUR WOMAN WILD IN BED
Staci Keith

*T*here's nothing like doing something sappy and adolescent to win her heart, so why not call a radio station and have them dedicate a song to your sweetheart? Every couple seems to have "their song" - one that, to them, perfectly epitomizes their feelings for each other. If you don't have one yet, pick one. And watch her heart strings quiver!

Q: If you wanted to tell your lover how much you care for her by playing one song, which song would you play and why?

46

LIGHT HER FIRE
Ellen Kreidman

*S*ex for her is kindness, gentleness, devotion, commitment, caring, patience, and compliments. It starts in the morning with whether you said "I love you" before you left. It's telling her how much she means to you. It's going shopping with her. It's helping her with chores. It's noticing that she has a new dress or hairdo. It's asking her to dinner. It's whether you phoned to say you'd be late. It's bringing home a card or a gift. Real romance for a woman is letting her know she's special, appreciated and loved. It's you spending time reaching out to her in a very giving way.

Unlike most men, a woman will not be in the mood to make love just because you are there. She'll be in the mood because you are nice to her.

Q: In what ways do you express love differently than your partner?

47

THE FOUR CORNERSTONES OF EROTICISM

Jack Moran

*S*exual arousal, whether it involves romance or pure lust, is highest when there is a tension between the attraction pulling us toward the partner, and one or more barriers standing in the way. The formula for hot sex is ATTRACTION + OBSTACLES = EXCITEMENT. The obstacles necessary for high excitement may be external or internal, conscious or unconscious. They can arouse us whenever something makes it difficult to get together. Or the chemistry between the partners can bring its own obstacles into the encounter. Overcoming barriers is a testament to the strength of the attraction.

Q: Jack Moran, a renowned clinical psychologist, has cooked up the following Erotic Equation:
Obstacles + Attraction = Hot Sex. How would *you* alter the equation to make it add up to even better sex?

48

HOT MONOGAMY
Dr. Patricia Love and Jo Robinson

*I*n one survey a thousand men were asked what turned them on most: dirty talk, x-rated videos, pornography, female masturbation, sexy lingerie, or "other." Of the men surveyed, 92% said they were most turned on by sexy lingerie. In an interesting footnote, 73% of these men said they relied on stimulation such as this to sustain their interest in a long-term relationship. In essence, a man who asks his partner to wear a lace teddy to bed may be saying to her, "Please help me be monogamous."

Q: Which type of lingerie literally makes your heart race? What totally turns you off?

49

MARS AND VENUS IN THE BEDROOM
John Gray, Ph.D.

*W*hen Mom said that the way to a man's heart was through his stomach she was about four inches too high. Sex is the direct line to a man's heart.

"Men Only Want One Thing"

Women commonly think men only want one thing: sex. The truth however, is that men really want love. A man wants love just as much as a woman, but before he can open his heart and let in his partner's love, sexual arousal is a prerequisite. Just as a woman needs love to open up to sex, a man needs sex to open up to love.

As a general guideline, a woman needs to be emotionally fulfilled before she can long for sexual contact. A man, however, gets much of his emotional fulfillment during sex.

Women do not understand this about men. The hidden reason a man is in such a hurry to have sex is that through sex, a man is able to feel again. Throughout the day, a man becomes so focused on his work that he loses touch with his loving feelings. Sex helps him to feel again. Through sex, a man's heart begins to open up. Through sex, a man can give and receive love the most.

Q: What does sex mean to you?

50

DAVE BARRY'S GUIDE TO MARRIAGE AND OR SEX
Dave Barry

*W*hat's the secret of a happy marriage? Call me a romantic if you want, but for me, the answer is the same simple, beautiful idea that has been making relationships work for thousands of years: separate bathrooms. You give two people room to spread out their toiletry articles, and you have the basis of a long-term relationship. But you make them perform their personal hygiene activities in the same small enclosed space, year in and year out, constantly finding the other person's bodily hairs stuck on their deodorant sticks, and I don't care how loving they were when they started out. I don't care if they were Ozzie and Harriet. They'll be slipping strychnine into each other's non-dairy creamer.

Of course even an ideal marriage, even a marriage where the bathrooms are 75 feet apart, is going to have a certain amount of conflict. This is because marriages generally involve males and females, which are not called "opposite sexes" for nothing.

Q: What's the secret to a happy marriage?

51

WILD IN BED TOGETHER
Graham Masterton

*W*hen he's making love, a great lover thinks only about arousing the woman in his arms, by any means possible, and about how much she excites him in return. Concentration is what makes a great lovers' lovemaking electric and everybody else's lovemaking ordinary. From the moment that he brings her to a stunning and satisfying orgasm, a great lover gives her the impression that he thinks and cares only about making her feel special.

Q: In general, how can women be better lovers?

52

THE TEN-SECOND KISS
Ellen Kreidman, Ph.D.

Do you know why so many relationships don't last? It's because the couples forget their plan of action. They forget what they did in the beginning.

- What they did was kiss.
- What they did was make each other feel special.
- What they did was talk.
- What they did was listen.
- What they did was hug.
- What they did was spend time alone together.

They fell in love because of their actions.

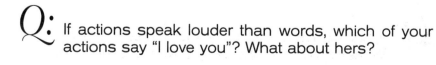

Q: If actions speak louder than words, which of your actions say "I love you"? What about hers?

53

WHAT MEN REALLY WANT
Susan Crain Bakos

*H*is is erotic variety. He wants something other than a dozen roses and a love note on the pillow.

As a columnist, I received hundreds of letters from men asking why wives or girlfriends wouldn't shave off their pubic hair; talk dirty in bed, make love in garter belt, black stockings, and high heels, or masturbate for them. The men in my survey harbored the same desires. Almost 90 percent of them rated more than one of these a turn-on and several wrote explaining why they craved stimuli women didn't.

Q: What do men find sexy that most women don't? What do women find sexy that most men don't?

54

THE DR. DREW AND ADAM BOOK

Drew Pinsky, M.D., and Adam Carolla

Q: What is most guys' biggest sexual fear?

Adam: Not getting enough of it. We do deal with people who have dysfunction, premature ejaculation. But I would say not getting any is the biggest fear.

Dr. Drew: That and penis size.

Adam: I think for a lot of guys it's plain old getting laid. You could take all the guys with questions about function and size and all that and it wouldn't amount to as many guys who are worried about not getting it.

Q. Is it normal for a guy to be insecure about his sexual performance?

Dr. Drew: Here's something we don't really acknowledge in the culture-- and that is that our sexuality is a big part of ourselves. That's who we are and how we experience ourselves. And most of us are pretty insecure about that, particularly as it pertains to our relations to others, which is what sex is. So it's natural enough that we should have insecurities there. Women are less insecure. They want to make sure the guy is happy-- that kind of thing. But guys are really concerned about it. Their identity is wrapped up in being able to adequately perform.

 *Q:* What sexual insecurities do you have?

55

1001 WAYS TO BE ROMANTIC (NEW & EXPANDED)
Gregory J.P. Godek

*H*e always did have a tendency to "overdo" things. One year he rented a limousine for her birthday. She enjoyed it so much that the following year he rented the limo again but this time he rented it for an entire week! So in addition to their fancy night on the town, she got chauffeured to the super market, to the dry cleaner, to church; the kids got chauffeured to school, to soccer practice, to the playground. A memorable experience for one and all!

Q: What is the most romantic thing anyone has ever done for you?

56

IT WAS ON FIRE WHEN I LAY DOWN ON IT
Robert Fulghum

*S*how-and-Tell was the very best part of school for me, both as a student and as a teacher. Not recess or lunch, but that special time set aside each week for students to bring something important of their own to class to share and talk about.

As a kid, I put more into getting ready for my turn to present then I put into the rest of my homework. Show-and-Tell was real in a way that much of what I learned in school was not. It was education that came out of my life experience. And there weren't a lot of rules about Show-and-Tell -- you could do your thing without getting red-penciled or gonged to your seat.

As a teacher, I was always surprised by what I learned from these amateur hours. A kid I was sure I knew well would reach down into the paper bag he carried and fish out some odd-shaped treasure and attach meaning to it beyond my most extravagant expectation. It was me, the teacher, who was being taught at such moments.

Q: Of all the gifts you have received, which one meant the most and why?

57

THE GUIDE TO GETTING IT ON
Paul Joannides

*I*t doesn't matter if you are a Christian, atheist, Moslem or Jew, we live in a country that was founded with a Bible in one hand and a firearm in the other. As a result, many of our society's values are rooted in a rather strange trining of gunpowder and holy scripture. Faith is important, but it never hurts to have a Smith & Wesson handy...

If you believe that religion has no influence over your daily life, grab your purse, wallet or conk your piggy bank over the head. Pull out any form of U.S. currency from a penny to a hundred dollar bill. Each piece of money bears two four-word phrases. One is "United States Of America." Check out the other.

Religious leaders have often ranted and railed against certain sexual practices, from masturbation and oral sex to homosexuality, as though these acts were the handiwork of the devil.

Q: Why is our society more comfortable with pain than pleasure? If we saw more acts of love and seduction than acts of violence on TV, how do you think our world would be different?

58

LIGHT HIS FIRE
Ellen Kreidman

*P*lanning a surprise for your mate is one very direct way to show that you really care and to create a memory at the same time. The one receiving the surprise only gets to enjoy it while it lasts or as a memory, but you'll have the added pleasure of planning and executing the entire event. I always tell women to plan an "Oh, no, I couldn't. That's not me" kind of surprise because when you do something that is completely out of character, your heart beats faster and your adrenaline flows. Do something unpredictable, spontaneous, and different. Don't worry that you're "not the type"-everyone has the ability to be creative and exciting. It just takes time, energy, and the willingness to try something different.

 Q: If you could receive a surprise package right before sex, what would be in it?

59

THE TEN-SECOND KISS
Ellen Kreidman, Ph.D.

*S*tarting today, I want you to touch your mate at least once a day. It doesn't matter whether you rub, tickle, scratch, massage, or caress your mate. What matters is that you touch each other every day.

I want one of the ways you touch during the week to be a twenty-second hug--not two seconds, not five seconds, not fifteen seconds--but a full twenty seconds! Timing is critical here. It takes at least five seconds to block out all the outside distractions and focus in on your mate. Once you've done that, it takes an additional fifteen seconds to stay in the present moment with your mate as you exchange loving energy.

When hugging, it is important to remember that not only are you giving, you are receiving. Just as with the ten-second kiss, when you engage in a twenty-second hug, you and your mate begin to breathe in unison with each other. You infuse each other with your life force as you become one. If you are concentrating only on giving, this sacred exchange of energy cannot take place.

When giving a hug, focus on sending love from your heart. When receiving a hug, focus on taking love in through your heart. If you take the time to feel both the giving and the receiving, your hug will nurture you, your mate, and your relationship.

Q: What's the difference between hugging your partner and holding your partner?

60

THE SENSUOUS MAN
By "M"

*T*he sighs and groans of ecstasy have faded away. You lie in your woman's arms. What fulfillment! What contentment! And, if you're like me, you're falling asleep, WAKE UP! Keep touching, fondling, and caressing her; don't roll over and turn away from your partner as if you were finished with her. Your touch now is more precious than ever. This is the time for closeness.

It is also the time for communication. Probably no other occasion is more suited for real communication than the moments following intercourse.

Q: What's the best thing anyone's ever said to you right after making love? And what's the one comment you'd most like to forget?

61

THE GUIDE TO GETTING IT ON
Paul Joannides

Liking His Licking

Some guys enjoy it if you lick and suck on their testicles when they are on all fours and you are on your back beneath them. The added benefit for you is that you get to rest your head on a pillow!

The Exquisite Brush Off

Get yourself a make-up brush or a Japanese bamboo artist's brush, have your cowboy spread his legs, and gently brush his inner thighs, testicles, penis and abdomen. Doing repeated circles around the outside of his balls can feel especially nice. The sensation is subtle, somewhere between a feather and a fingertip. It can feel relaxing and titillating at the same time. If you enjoy a bit of bondage, tie him up first. After about thirty minutes of this, a guy might actually come from the brush strokes alone.

When brushing a guy off, don't limit your strokes to just his genitals. Try his face, back, feet and hands. If you're lucky, he'll grab the brush and return the favor.

Q: What kind of foreplay would you like to have that you're not getting now?

62

WHAT YOUR MOTHER COULDN'T TELL YOU AND YOUR FATHER DIDN'T KNOW

John Gray, Ph.D.

Honey Do's

"**W**hen I get home I am barraged with a list of 'honey do's,'" Sam groused. "As soon as I sit down, Lisa starts giving orders. It is like she waits for me to relax and then she needs more. When I get home, I feel like I have to hide from her. It is not just me, because when I talk to other men they also feel this way about their wives. I don't want to come home to another boss. I have to go on fishing trips just to get away."

Women don't realize that men need to relax and do nothing responsible for a while in order to recover from the day's stress. Particularly when she is overwhelmed, a woman feels that everything has to be done before she can relax. She mistakenly assumes that if she reminds her mate of what to do, then they will both eventually be able to relax.

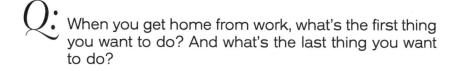

Q: When you get home from work, what's the first thing you want to do? And what's the last thing you want to do?

63

THE GUIDE TO GETTING IT ON
Paul Joannides

*W*hile bisexual women might be shunned by ardent lesbians, they fare much better overall than do bisexual men. For instance, a former hit song by a female singer named Jill Sobule is all about how she kissed a girl. Do you think that a song like this would have even been cut, let alone become popular in the straight community if it had been titled "I Kissed A Guy" and had been performed by a male singer? Perhaps one reason for the discrepancy is because a large number of straight males get off on the notion of two women making love, with a common fantasy being to watch their wives or girlfriends make it with another woman. On the other hand, not many women fantasize about their husbands making it with another man.

Q: You just won the sex lottery! You're single, unattached, and you get to go to bed with two famous people simultaneously. Who are they?

64

DAVE BARRY'S GUIDE TO GUYS
Dave Barry

Guys vs. Men

*T*HIS IS A BOOK about *guys*. It's not a book about men. There are already way too many books about men, and most of them are way too serious.

Men itself is a serious word, not to mention manhood and manly. Such words make being male sound like a very important activity, as opposed to what it primarily consists of, namely, possessing a set of minor and frequently unreliable organs.

But men tend to attach great significance to Manhood. This results in certain characteristically masculine, by which I mean stupid, behavioral patterns that can produce unfortunate results such as violent crime, war, spitting, and ice hockey. These things have given men a bad name. And the "Men's Movement," which is suppose to bring out the more positive aspects of Manliness, seems to be densely populated with loons and goobers.

So I'm saying that there's another way to look at males not as aggressive macho dominators, not as sensitive, liberated, hugging drummers, but as guys. And what, exactly, do I mean by "guys"? I don't know. I haven't thought that much about it.

Q: If you had to draw a pie chart of your personality, how much of you is: Macho Man, Mr. A-Hole, Regular Guy, and Sensitive Soul? How do you think your lover would divide you up?

65

SECRETS OF WORLD CLASS LOVERS

Jaid Barrymore

*J*ust thinking about the intimacy of the afterglow of orgasm brings an immediate smile to my face. How do I enjoy it? Let me count the ways. First of all, it's nice to just lie there in your lover's arms and savor the moment with soft language, kisses and caresses. Then, if either of you feels like moving, a cold glass of juice or a glass of wine can be the perfect thing to quench your thirst.

Perhaps by this time you're beginning to get the munchies. Maybe you'd like something a bit sweet—a piece of chocolate, a bite of cake with luscious whipped cream frosting, apple pie a' la mode, a bit of juicy fruit. Passion fruit, mangoes or kiwi are among my favorites. Or try peeling an orange or grapefruit and feeding sections of it to your lover. Rub the juice all over his body and then seductively lick it off. A bit of honey poured on your honey's body can be an equally tasty treat. Or dip grapes in that honey and place them between your lover's toes. Mmm, delicious.

Q: What's the most amazing thing a woman has ever done for you right after having sex?

66

WHAT TURNS MEN ON
Brigitte Nioche

Why aren't women aware of the power they have over men?

*I*f you doubt that we have power, just think of the men you know who worship their wives or lovers. Have you ever asked yourself why he adores her? Or did you think that she was just lucky to find such a loving man? In most cases luck doesn't have much to do with it. What you are looking at is a sexually satisfied man whose woman knows how to please him. She uses her sexual powers to bewitch him.

Q: It's been said that women "hold all the world's power between their legs." Why do you think women's sexuality weaves such a hypnotic spell over men? How has this sexual magic shaped your own life?

67

THE GUIDE TO GETTING IT ON
Paul Joannides

*D*ear Dr. Goofy,

My husband of fifteen years is the most trustworthy and hardworking man on the face of the earth. He's a great father to our kids and I love him dearly, but the romance in our relationship is gone. I can't remember the last time I received flowers from him that weren't for Mother's Day. The big trouble is, I've been noticing the pool man a lot more than I should. He compliments me on what I am wearing, asks me about the projects I am working on, and makes me laugh. By the time he leaves every Wednesday, I find myself wetter than the pool deck! It's not that he's some sort of physical ten or that we've had sexual contact, it's just his wonderful attitude and the way he takes the time to notice me. How do I get my husband to do the same?

Q: What is the highest compliment you can pay your lover?

68

THE TEN-SECOND KISS
Ellen Kreidman, Ph.D.

I wish I could give you the same sense of urgency that I feel. You do not know how much time you have left to love your mate the way he or she deserves to be loved. Don't let another day go by without putting into action the *KISS Plan* presented here:

- Kiss for at least ten seconds every day.
- Compliment at least one thing your mate has said or done every day.
- Talk and listen to each other for thirty minutes---every day.
- Hug for twenty seconds every day.
- Stay connected sexually.
- Plan a fantasy for each other.
- Make love on the spur of the moment.
- Laugh together every day.
- Make all your decisions based on love.

We are here for such a short time that it is imperative to make that time count. Don't live a life filled with regrets. Love like there's no tomorrow, because in the end love is the only thing that counts.

Q: How do you keep the romance alive in your relationship?

69

THE HITE REPORT
Shere Hite

*M*ost men felt guilty and inadequate about masturbating, at the same time that they enjoyed it tremendously (many had their strongest orgasms, physically, during masturbation). And seemed to have a great sense of freedom and fun while doing it. Most men seemed to feel freer to stimulate themselves in ways they liked, and to experiment, than at other times – to simply play around and be affectionate with their bodies. Almost no men told anyone else that they did this.

Most men, even though they continued to masturbate regularly throughout their lives, including many times during which they had and otherwise active sex life, felt that they should not masturbate, and that masturbation was basically acceptable for a man only as a substitute for sex with another person – many adding that they felt defensive, lonely, or guilty about doing it.

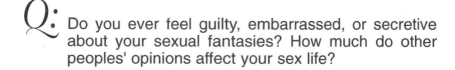

Q: Do you ever feel guilty, embarrassed, or secretive about your sexual fantasies? How much do other peoples' opinions affect your sex life?

70

HOT SEX
Tracey Cox

"*I*t's totally normal to continue masturbating even if you're living with a girl and have a fantastic sex life. Masturbation is one form of sex. It provides different feelings than sex with another person, so even if you're getting heaps of it with her, you still crave that different sensation. The only problem usually is opportunity. My (now ex) wife once caught me masturbating in the shower and was horrified. I thought at the time it was because she thought masturbating was dirty but I realize now it was because I wasn't having sex with her. She couldn't understand why I'd prefer to do it myself when she was lying in the next room."

- Gary

Q: Most men masturbate even when they're in a committed relationship. How does solo sex affect your sex life with your partner?

71

THE GUIDE TO GETTING IT ON
Paul Joannides

*A*lot of women have never seen a man masturbate, nor have many men seen a woman masturbate. Yet plenty of us, male or female, would find it interesting if not highly erotic to watch a partner masturbate.

In Front Of A Partner

For straight people, masturbating in front of a partner can sometimes take a lot of trust. That's because masturbation tends to be more self-disclosing than other types of sex. It can also leave you feeling vulnerable if your partner finds you doing it. ("Oh, hi honey, I was just sitting here playing with myself.") Still, most of us continue to masturbate even when we are in a relationship, and being open about it usually helps to expand sexual enjoyment for both partners.

There is often something erotic and even forbidden about seeing your partner masturbate. This is just as true for women watching men as for men watching women.

If your partner can see how you please yourself, it might help him or her understand more about pleasing you.

Orgasms from masturbation are often the most intense kind of orgasm. It might increase the level of intimacy in your relationship if you can ask your partner to hold you while you bring yourself to orgasm.

Q: Would you consider mutual masturbation to orgasm with your partner a night of great sex?

72

REAL AGE
Michael Roizen, M.D.

*T*his book is about getting younger. But what are we getting younger for? To enjoy life more. One of those enjoyments is sex. Sex keeps us young and makes us want to stay young. It's one of life's greatest pleasures, and not one that we want to give up because we're too old. Emotionally, physically, and mentally, remaining sexually active will help make your RealAge younger no matter what your calendar age. Why? It decreases stress, relaxes us, enhances intimacy, and helps form the foundation of strong and supportive personal relationships. No matter what your calendar age, nineteen or ninety, sex is a first rate age reducer.

Q: How much is your outlook on life and sense of well being affected by how much sex you're getting? What's the longest you've ever gone without making love?

73

SEX SECRETS OF THE OTHER WOMAN
Graham Masterson

*N*ight after night, all over the nation, couples are lying next to each other, needing each other, wanting each other, yet unable to communicate their desire by word or by gesture. A greater tragedy of noncommunication happens every night in this nation's marriage beds than all the years of the Cold War put together.

It's impossible to say by how much the divorce rate could be reduced by better sexual communication. But there is no question that millions of potentially happy marriages are marred forever by nothing more dramatic than the inability of husbands and wives to discuss their sexual needs together.

Q: Why is it so difficult to talk about your sexual needs?

74

DRIVE HIM WILD
Graham Masterton

*W*omen need physical stimulation and regular climaxes in order to be sexually satisfied.

They need affection, warmth, reassurance, security, and a sense of masculine strength.

But they also need a sense of excitement -- even a sense of sexual danger. They need creative and colorful sex -- the sex of fantasy and romance.

Literally scores of women have told me about fantasies that closely resemble Marion's. In each case, they have been naked in front of dozens of purient eyes-either posing or masturbating or making love. It seems clear that many women have a strong element of exhibitionism in their sexual makeup, and that they are very aroused by the idea of showing themselves off sexually to an audience.

Q: If you were forced to name the one aspect of your own sexuality that you least understand, what would it be?

75

5 MINUTES TO ORGASM

D. Claire Hutchins

*S*ince the studies of Masters and Johnson, it has been well known that women have orgasms during sex because of clitoral stimulation, regardless of whether they are aware of the stimulation (masturbation, vibrators, or oral sex) or not (pulling and rubbing of the clitoral "hood" by the thrusting penis). Though this knowledge is often hidden in popular wisdom, educated and sexually confident women must reject the theory that manual stimulation of the clitoris during sex is abnormal, unnecessary, or sick.

All major studies of female sexuality subsequent to Masters and Johnson support that women do not automatically have orgasms during intercourse – from intercourse – from simple thrusting of the penis. Yet millions of women enjoy orgasm while the man's penis is within the vagina by using additional stimulation of the clitoris. The question should not be, is this wrong? Can this be fixed? The question should be, why do we keep asking such a stupid question in the first place? Why resort to everything in the book, from scented candles and coed bubble baths, to extensive analysis and sex therapy to MAKE orgasm happen any other way? Ladies – let's move on!

If the thought of touching yourself in front of your partner scares you, you'll have to get over it.

Q: How would it make you feel if your lover could not reach orgasm during intercourse without some form of manual clitoral stimulation?

76

IN THE MOOD
Doreen Virtue, Ph.D.

*H*ere's a list of the actions most often cited by men as turn-ons leading to romantic mood, listed in order from most to least frequent:

1. Being with a woman who looks good or dresses seductively
2. A home-cooked dinner
3. Non-sexual touching, such as hugging, massaging, or caressing
4. Eye contact or a special way of looking at each other
5. Low lights or candlelight
6. Having a partner who makes a special effort to make a romantic evening
7. Having a partner who is spontaneous or who surprises me
8. Kissing
9. Soft music
10. Wine or champagne
11. A woman who smells great
12. A quiet atmosphere

All these turn-ons strike me as gentle, tender expressions of male and female bonding. A romantic setting is very important to a man —- he enjoys dimmed lights, soft music and a quiet atmosphere. His romantic mood is aroused when his female partner puts a special effort into making him feel like a king.

Q: If you wanted to turn your lover on as quickly as possible, what would you do?

77

203 WAYS TO DRIVE A MAN WILD IN BED
Olivia St. Claire

*F*ew things turn a man on more than a lusty woman showing him how much she's enjoying herself, how much his thrusting penis is turning her on. So let your passion show. Moan and groan with pleasure. Pant with excitement. Wriggle with abandon because you're so hot you just can't keep still. Nuzzle him appreciatively. Parry his thrusts eagerly. Wrap you legs around him and squeeze. Grab his bottom and push him into you with each thrust as if you can't get enough of him. Gently scratch and bit; he'll be proud to bear the scars of your passion. Vibrate. Scream. Grind. Toss and turn. Lick, kiss, and suck him as if you'd like to swallow him whole. Each move, each sound, each sensation will magnify his excitement and spur him on to even more fabulous lovemaking. And don't forget to . . .

Tell him how excited you feel. Earlier, I touted the benefits of verbal foreplay, but now that the game is in full swing, you can really get down to talking "dirty."

Q: If a woman wanted to intensify your orgasm, what words should she whisper in your ear *right before* you climax?

78

5 MINUTES TO ORGASM
D. Claire Hutchins

*W*hile extremely long, drawn-out lovemaking sessions are wonderful in a fledgling relationship, after a while it can seem like too much work. Even worse, a man's continual thrusting in and out of a woman's vagina in an effort to help her reach orgasm, can actually hurt. A prolonged sexual encounter can be agony for the woman, but men don't always realize this. I've heard men brag that they can "go all night." Sometimes they wear this "skill" like a badge of honor. They don't realize that women are not sexual perpetual motion machines; it is fairly easy to get to the point where stimulation actually hurts.

Women can't and don't want to go on forever. No wonder the glamour quickly goes out of the marriage bed. It is not surprising that women would rather go out to dinner than have sex.

Q: If it were entirely up to you, your sex sessions--from foreplay to climax--would last how long?

79

HOT AND BOTHERED
Wendy Dennis

*W*hat do women love in bed?

Well, no big surprises here. Women love a lover with a slow touch. First they a love titillating verbal seduction ("He has to f**k my head before he f**ks me," one woman put it), and then they love a gradual physical seduction. What this means is that they love being undressed adoringly, and caressed from the top of their heads to the tips of their toes. On the other hand, sometimes they just love being bent over and plowed, so go figure.

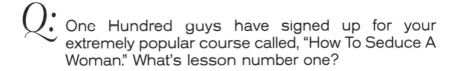

Q: One Hundred guys have signed up for your extremely popular course called, "How To Seduce A Woman." What's lesson number one?

80

WHAT MEN REALLY WANT
Susan Crain Bakos

*S*ex in semipublic places is high on the male wish list. They want to do it on the balcony or patio, in bathrooms or closets at parties, in your childhood bed while visiting Mom and Dad. What's a close second to the fantasy of intercourse on a plane or train, a Forum readers' favorite? Having her perform fellatio while he's driving on an interstate highway. Partly he craves the visual thrill of watching her do something she wouldn't do without being coaxed. And partly the risk of getting caught arouses him.

 Where is the zaniest, most unusual place you would like to make love...but haven't?

81

THE GUIDE TO GETTING IT ON
Paul Joannides

Toys, Pain & Pleasure

*A*s a woman, the first thing you will find out about penises (and testicles) is that most guys take them way too seriously. There are reasons for this:

- The penis is the only childhood toy that a guy gets to keep and play with throughout his entire life. It is the only toy he will ever own that feels good when he tugs on it, it constantly changes size and shape, and it is activated by the realm of the senses. Try to find that at Toys"R'Us.

- One of the first things a man does when he wakes up in the morning and the last thing he does at night is to touch his penis and testicles. It is a male ritual of self-affirmation that has little to do with sexual stimulation. A daytime extension known as pocket pool.

Q: The old saying goes, "When you die, the boy with most toys wins." What's *your* motto?

82

HOT SEX
Tracey Cox

In reality, the more sexually active you are, the more likely you are to masturbate, regardless of whether you do or don't have a partner. Kinsey, the world's best known sex expert, found that women who have a history of masturbating are more likely to easily experience orgasm later in life with a partner. They also tend to have fewer sexual problems than women who don't indulge.

This is one area where men are ahead. Most women masturbate about once a week, often not doing it regularly until their late teens. Most men masturbate at least twice as often, and started doing so around twelve or thirteen years of age. Of the women who have discovered its joys, virtually all can masturbate to orgasm--95 percent of us, in fact (and some researchers put that figure even higher). On the opposite side, if you're a female who has never masturbated, statistics indicate it's quite likely you've never had an orgasm in your life. Pretty strong support for solo sex!

Q: Have you ever been caught masturbating? If so, by whom?

83

WHY MEN DON'T GET ENOUGH SEX AND WOMEN DON'T GET ENOUGH LOVE

Jonathan Krarner, Ph.D./Diane Dunaway

Some men like the naughty girl image of black and red or leather. Others prefer the sweet girl-next-door image. Decide what he will like best or vary your images. Remember not to be predictable. Do something he does not expect. Do something daring, even slightly dangerous or forbidden. He may not entirely approve, but it will probably excite him anyway.

Besides, men don't leave women for being sexy, unpredictable, and slightly dangerous. They leave them for being boring.

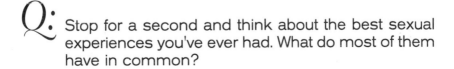

$Q{:}$ Stop for a second and think about the best sexual experiences you've ever had. What do most of them have in common?

84

TANTRIC SEX
E.J. Gold and Cybele Gold

*D*uring the course of your ordinary sex, break contact before either of you is able to have an orgasm.

Immediately withdraw physical contact, quietly get dressed, and do something else together. Anything but sex.

Q: Do you believe that stopping intercourse just short of orgasm can build anticipation that will lead to a more exciting orgasm at a later time?

85

WHY MEN STRAY AND WHY MEN STRAY
Alexandra Penny

*I*f I asked you, "Quick! Name the three things your lover likes most when you make love," you should be able to answer that question as fast as you can recite your ABC's, but the fact is that many women can't. Even though we may know exactly what our husbands desire for dinner, we aren't nearly as sure about what satisfies their appetites in bed. If you're not meeting his sexual needs, by now you should know just how much trouble that can lead to.

Q: Name three things you should *always* do to a woman while making love. On the flip side, what should you *never* do?

86

THE SENSUOUS WOMAN
By "J"

*W*hen you have educated your body to the point where it can reel off several orgasms at your command, you will be able to guide him, when you are making love to positions that give you the maximum sensation. After all, if **you** don't know what sets your body off sensually, how can you expect **him** to know? Every woman is different and he's not clairvoyant.

Q: Who's responsible for the female orgasm?

87

MEN ARE FROM MARS, WOMEN ARE FROM VENUS
John Gray, Ph.D.

Little Things Make A Big Difference

*S*ome men may start out in a relationship doing the little things, but having done them once or twice they stop. Through some mysterious instinctive force, they begin to focus their energies into doing one big thing for their partners. They then neglect to do all the little things that are necessary for a woman to feel fulfilled in the relationship. To fulfill a woman, a man needs to understand what she needs to feel loved and supported.

The way women score points is not just a preference but a true need. Women need many expressions of love in a relationship to feel loved. One or two expressions of love, no matter how important, will not, and cannot, fulfill her.

This can be extremely hard for a man to understand. One way to look at it is to imagine that women have a love tank similar to the gas tank on a car. It needs to be filled over and over again. Doing many little things (and scoring many points) is the secret for filling a woman's love tank. A woman feels loved when her love tank is full. She is able to respond with greater love, trust, acceptance, appreciation, admiration, approval, and encouragement. Lots of little things are needed to top off her tank.

Q: What are three little things you can do through out the day to really put her in the mood?

88

THE GUIDE TO GETTING IT ON
Paul Joannides

Telling Children About Sexual Enjoyment

*P*arents usually tell their children all there is to know about things like blowing noses and wiping rear ends, but rarely do they mention that genitals can be the source of good feelings. As a result, children learn that it's OK to seek their parents' wisdom on just about everything but sexual feelings. This is most unfortunate, because kids need their parents' guidance on sexual feelings as much as they do on wiping their rear ends or learning to drive a car.

Some parents assume that a three-year-old who is rubbing her genitals has the same intent and fantasies as a twenty-three-year-old. They either try to stop her or simply pretend that nothing is happening. Perhaps it would be helpful for parents to understand that their masturbating three-year-old isn't thinking about how good Johnnie, her daycare buddy, might be in bed! The child is simply touching her genitals, because it feels good. It is perfectly normal for little hands to reach between little legs when a child is happy, excited, at naptime or even when you are reading Dr. Seuss to them.

Q: In what ways have your parents' behaviors and attitudes toward sex influenced or affected your own sexuality?

89

203 WAYS TO DRIVE A MAN WILD IN BED
Olivia St. Claire

*T*he foot fetish - During intercourse, whenever you're in a position to reach his feet easily, you might consider this little trick. Just as he's about to have his orgasm, grasp his toes and pull gently. It seems that a man's toe bone is connected to his genital bone, and this extra stimulation increases the intensity of his ejaculation.

Q: If your lover wanted to double your pleasure, what two sexy things should she do to you at the same time?

90

THE GUIDE TO GETTING IT ON
Paul Joannides

*A*dding A Squeeze Or Twist. — Try giving a well-lubricated hand job where your entire hand wraps around the penis and twists up and down it as though it were following the red stripe on a barber's pole. Try a similar twisting motion with your head during oral sex (just a slight turn of the neck is all that's needed, nothing to give you whiplash). At the same time, work the area between his testicles with one of your hands.

Q: In the last decade, there has been a onslaught of sexual how-to books and videos. What have you learned from this kind of material, and when was the last time you tried one of these techniques with your partner?

91

MEN ARE FROM MARS, WOMEN ARE FROM VENUS
John Gray, Ph.D.

The Art of Empowering a Man

*J*ust as men need to learn the art of listening to fulfill a woman's primary love needs, women need to learn the art of empowerment. When a woman enlists the support of a man, she empowers him to be all that he can be. A man feels empowered when he is trusted, accepted, appreciated, admired, approved of, and encouraged.

Like in our story of the knight in shining armor, many women try to help their man by improving him but unknowingly weaken or hurt him. Any attempt to change him takes away the loving trust, acceptance, appreciation, admiration, approval, and encouragement that are his primary needs.

Q: What is it about love that makes you most afraid?

92

MARS AND VENUS IN THE BEDROOM
John Gray, Ph.D.

Going to Cultural to Events

Grant still remembers when he first recognized the importance of cultural events for creating romance. It was before he started taking charge of these matters. After hinting around for a while about going to the symphony, Theresa went ahead and bought tickets for them to go.

It was a great concert, and afterward when they were driving home, she greatly surprised him. He knew she had liked it, but he didn't realize how much.

She said, "Thanks so much for taking me. It was so good." Then, after a pause, she said, "I'm feeling really wet."

He said, "Wet?"

She nodded. "Yeah."

He got so excited that when they got home and into their own garage, they took off their clothes and did it in the car.

Needless to say, the next morning Grant got up early and called to get season tickets to the symphony.

 Q: What's the most sexually spontaneous thing you have ever done? How about the most adventurous?

93

THE GUIDE TO GETTING IT ON
Paul Joannides

Your Lover's Sex Fantasies

*E*very once in a while, one partner will tell the other about his or her private sex fantasy. (Stranger things have happened.) But don't expect to see the fantasy plastered on a billboard surrounded by neon lights. Most of us are a little embarrassed by our sexual fantasies, sometimes with good reason. As a result, we tend not to reveal our sex fantasies in a way that's particularly direct.

Q: You just won a contest on your favorite radio station. The prize? A massive billboard right in the heart of your city. It's yours for thirty days with only one catch: Your message has to make women smile. What will you have it say?

94

MEN ARE FROM MARS, WOMEN ARE FROM VENUS
John Gray, Ph.D.

*G*oing Out With the Guys

Each week, Craig has a ritual of going to the movies or doing something with his male friends. They generally go and see a "guy" movie, the kind of movie his wife, Sarah, doesn't like.

Although at first this kind of ritual may not seem support their relationship, but it does. Spending time with the guys keeps him from expecting to get all his support from Sarah. Time away helps him to feel completely free to be himself. As a result, he begins to miss her and want to be with her even more.

Sarah understands this because she greatly appreciates the support he gives her to spend time with her women friends. He recognizes that it is eventually important for her to get many of her needs met by women friends so that she is not looking to him for everything.

When he goes out with the guys, her accepting attitude about it really makes him feel her support. It used to be that she would look at him in a hurt way whenever he went out with the guys. Now she even reminds him to go out when he forgets.

Q: When you're with your male friends, what do they say about women – both good and bad?

95

WHAT YOUR MOTHER COULDN'T TELL YOU AND YOUR FATHER DIDN'T KNOW
John Gray, Ph.D.

*W*hen a man loves a woman, his primary goal is to make her happy. Through history, men have endured the competitive and hostile world work because, at the end of the day, their struggles and efforts were justified by a woman's appreciation. In a very real sense, his mate's fulfillment was the reward that made a man's labor worthwhile.

Today, because women are overworked, they often and understandably feel unfulfilled. Now, at a long day's end, both she and her mate are looking for love and appreciation. "I work as hard as he does," she tells herself. "Why is it my responsibility to appreciate him?" Exhaustion now prevents her from giving her man the emotional support she knows he's earned. If a man is not appreciated, he feels his work is meaningless; his wife's unhappiness confirms his defeat. To him, her unhappiness signals that he is a failure. "Why should I bother to do more?" he asks himself "I'm unappreciated for what I do already." The harmful effects of this relatively new pattern are greatly underestimated by both women and men.

Q: With jobs, kids, chores, and the demands of day-to-day life, it can sometimes seem impossible to keep the passion alive. Whose responsibility is it to keep the music playing?

96

LIGHT HIS FIRE
Ellen Kreidman

*Y*our Hero Forever

For every action there is a reaction. For every trait there is a response to that trait. You must learn to react in a positive way and stop being judgmental. When you concentrate on a man's strengths instead of his weaknesses, you get more positive behavior.

It's been said, "Women always marry a man and hope he'll change. Men always marry a woman and hope she'll never change."

Women seem to go into a relationship saying, "I know there are a lot of things about him that I don't like, but wait until I get through with him. You won't even recognize him."

Men, on the other hand, say, "when I'm with this woman, I feel like a king. It's wonderful. I hope she never changes. I always want to feel like this." That, by the way, is why he wants to marry this woman. He wants to feel like her hero for the rest of her life.

Once you begin to focus on all the things you consider weaknesses and try to change him, the love you had in the beginning starts to die.

Q: What's your definition of a man who's been completely "pussified"? In what ways do women try to "pussify" men?

97

HIS NEEDS, HER NEEDS

Willard F. Harley, Jr.

The First Thing He Can't Do Without—Sexual Fulfillment.

A man cannot achieve fulfillment in his marriage unless his wife is sexually fulfilled as well. While I have maintained that men need sex more than women, unless a woman joins her husband in the sexual experience, his need for sex remains unmet. Therefore, a woman does her husband no favors by sacrificing her body to his sexual advances. He can feel sexually satisfied only when she joins him in the experience of lovemaking.

Q: Would an unsatisfying sex life without hope of improvement cause you to dissolve a relationship? How long could you go without sexual intercourse and still preserve a healthy relationship?

98

SEX AND HUMAN LOVING
Masters and Johnson

*D*on't be trapped into thinking that sex has always got to include intercourse to be meaningful or gratifying. By occasionally omitting intercourse from a lovemaking session, you may even discover other pleasures that are equally arousing.

Q: Should every sexual encounter with your partner include intercourse?

99

5 MINUTES TO ORGASM
D. Claire Hutchins

*T*oday's most popular syndicated radio personality has shared on his morning show how he feels about his wife's vibrator. When they have sex, he claims, he must use it on her before she can achieve orgasm. He typically complains that she's starting to take longer to reach orgasm even with the vibrator. He resents the extra work. He complains that she is getting a callous "down there."

Although research indicates that some women find a vibrator enjoyable, some find it painful, annoying and distracting. While it can be an occasional source of fun and variety, when it becomes an expediter to bring a woman to orgasm quickly and save time, problems may result. Female orgasm should be simple, but for many it has become a chore. I have no objection to oral sex and vibrators at all – unless they are always used as a replacement for the sex act and if partners think they have no other choice. Orgasm through cunnilingus and vibrators is fulfilling, at least for the recipient. But the man's penis is not inside you, and you are not having intercourse. Only the most determined of romantics could find this scenario exciting day after day, year after year.

Q: If your lover couldn't have an orgasm without the help of a sex toy, how would that make you feel?

100

NICE GIRLS DO
Dr. Irene Kassoria

*C*ontrary to popular belief, increased sensuality offers increased safety to a relationship. As a woman becomes more sensual, she will feel more confident with herself and safer in the relationship.

Many scientific studies have found that women who are sensual and orgasm more frequently, tend also to be more successful, more motivated in their work, and are more able to express feelings of heightened self-worth and self-esteem.

Q: What makes a woman truly sensuous?

101

MEN ARE FROM MARS, WOMEN ARE FROM VENUS
John Gray, Ph.D.

Love Motivates Martians

*M*ost men are not only hungry to give love but are starving for it. Their biggest problem is that they do not know what they are missing. They rarely saw their fathers succeed in fulfilling their mothers through giving. As a result they do not know that a major source of fulfillment for a man can come through giving. When his relationships fail he finds himself depressed and stuck in his cave. He stops caring and doesn't know why he is so depressed.

At such times he withdraws from relationships or intimacy and remains stuck in his cave. He asks himself what it is all for, and why he should bother. He doesn't know that he has stopped caring because he doesn't feel needed. He does not realize that by finding someone who needs him, he can shake off his depression and be motivated again.

When a man doesn't feel he is making a positive difference in someone else's life, it is hard for him to continue caring about his life and relationships. It is difficult to be motivated when he is not needed. To become motivated again he needs to feel appreciated, trusted, and accepted.

Not To Be Needed Is A Slow Death For A Man

Q: How important is it for you to feel needed?

102

SECRETS OF THE SEXUALLY IRRESISTIBLE WOMAN
Graham Masterton

I talked to over 120 divorced and separated men about the reasons they had been unfaithful to their partners. Of course, simple incompatibility was a major factor—"She's a vegetarian but I can't do without my baby back ribs," "We were high school sweethearts but we just grew up, and when we grew up we grew apart."

But one of the main reasons they looked elsewhere was because they believed that the women in their lives weren't sufficiently interested in sex. " I came home late, feeling as horny as an antelope, and all she did was turn her back on me." "I tried to kiss her but she said my breath smelled of drink, and then I tried to go down on her, but she said my chin was too stubbly...so, in the end, I turned over and said forget it." And the most common complaint of all: "She was frigid, that's the top and bottom of it...she just didn't like sex."

Q: When 100,000 men were asked "Have you ever had an extramarital affair?" during a recent survey, a whopping seventy-eight percent said yes! Why do you think so many men have a hard time being monogamous?

103

1001 WAYS TO BE ROMANTIC
Gregory J.P. Godek

*M*any men would consider this the Ultimate Gift: A "Fantasy Photo" of you. You can get a sensual, provocative and stunning "Fantasy Portrait" made of yourself by contacting a photographer who specializes in the growing art form often called "Boudoir Photographer." Many of these photographers are women with a talent for making their subjects feel comfortable, and then bringing out the subtle, sexy side of your personality, and capturing it on film. "Lingerie" portraits seem to be the most popular, followed by "Fantasy Outfit" shots and nude photography.

Q: Your lover has agreed to do anything for the camera, anything at all - as long as *you* are the photographer. What kind of picture will you take?

104

REAL MOMENTS FOR LOVERS
Barbara De Angelis, Ph.D.

*Y*our eyes don't merely see -- they give off energy. Have you ever had someone give you a look that made you tingle all over with pleasure, or made you feel as if you'd been stabbed with daggers, or filled you up with strength and courage? Their eyes didn't just passively see you-they passed an energy to you, an energy you took in through your eyes.

In this same way, how you use your eyes in your relationship can have a positive or negative effect on your partner. Each glance you send his or her way can create more love, or more mistrust and distance, between you. You won't have to say anything -- he will feel loved or not loved by the way you look at him. Your eyes cannot lie.

Q: When you're out with a woman, do you only have eyes for her? Do you expect her to only have eyes for you?

105

THE DR. DREW AND ADAM BOOK
Drew Pinsky, M.D., and Adam Carolla

Q: If you find out a partner has been cheating, should you stay or should you go?

Dr. Drew: If you can't trust them, you can't reestablish the relationship because you're not going to be open to them.

Look at your own family system. If you come from a system where cheating is accepted, get some treatment because it's not going to stop. That model is emblazoned in your head: that men can just behave that way. But that's not the way guys should be. It's the way women allow them to be.

If a person is clear that it was an absolute, categorical mistake, that it was some kind of extraordinary circumstance, and if forgiveness is possible, then the relationship can probably move forward on a basis of honesty. In an ideal relationship, it's better for all the information to be available. There's a saying in Alcoholics Anonymous: "You're as sick as your secrets." The more an individual hides who he is, the less truth there is. For a relationship to be healthy, there needs to be as much truth as possible about who these people are in the relationship for the relationship to be genuine and real. Yes, it's painful to deal with the truth—but that's the road to health.

Adam: You have to decide two things: Is this person likely to do it again? And am I going to hold it against this person? If the answer is yes to either one of those questions, you can't get back together. If they're going to cheat or you suspect they're going to cheat, you can't get back together. If you can't forgive them and will never stop holding this against them, you can't get together.

Q: Under what circumstances, if any, could you forgive infidelity and continue the relationship?

106

THE ROAD LESS TRAVELED
M. Scott Peck, M.D.

*S*ince true listening is love in action, nowhere is it more appropriate than in marriage. Yet most couples never truly listen to each other. Consequently, when couples come to us for counseling or therapy, a major task we must accomplish if the process is to be successful is to teach them how to listen. Not infrequently we fail, the energy and discipline involved being more than they are willing to expend or submit themselves to. Couples are often surprised, even horrified, when we suggest to them that among the things they should do is talk to each other by appointment. It seems rigid and unromantic and unspontaneous to them. Yet true listening can occur only when time is set aside for it and conditions are supportive of it. It cannot occur when people are driving, or cooking or tired and anxious to sleep or easily interrupted or in a hurry. Romantic "love" is effortless, and couples are frequently reluctant to shoulder the effort and discipline of true love and listening.

But when and if they finally do, the results are superbly gratifying.

Q: In your relationship, do you do more listening or talking?

107

IN THE MOOD
Doreen Virtue, Ph.D.

*B*y taking the time to look attractive, you are speaking volumes of love to your man. Then, after you look great, be sure to look at your man. He needs your eye contract while he's talking, just as much as you need him to tell you that he loves you. Give him your full attention, as you did on your first date. Smile at him and laugh at his jokes. You're not being passive or manipulative by engaging in this nonverbal communication. You're simply speaking his language!

Q: How important do you think flirting with your partner is in a long-term relationship? What's the one flirty thing she does that makes your heart skip-a-beat?

108

203 WAYS TO DRIVE A MAN WILD IN BED
Olivia St. Claire

Secret #3: Concentrate on Him.

Women who make sex their profession know the surest and most direct way to a man's libido. They focus their attention completely on him, and only him. So take a tip from the pros.

Forget about the disagreement you had with the boss earlier. Don't waste time and energy worrying whether your hair looks effectively mussed – or whether your hand isn't better off on his knee than on his elbow. Focus your attention on him; his manly chest, his adorable derriere, his playful penis. Make him feel that no one else exists for you but him. No one could possibly be a better, more exciting lover than he is. Let him see that he has truly swept you away with desire.

When you forget yourself and start concentrating instead on your man, you'll find yourself automatically doing wonderfully provocative things to him. They will come naturally to you because of your heightened sexual awareness. You'll do just the things that excite him, not because you have to or because you've painstakingly selected them from your mental bag of sex tricks, but because you just want to.

Forget about your own pleasure and focus only his. What con you do to make him feel wanted? Relaxed? Sexy? Soothed? Ecstatic? As if you can't get enough of him? Fondle him. Caress him. Kiss him lavishly. Lick and nibble him all over. Tell him he's handsome. Strong. Hard. Irresistible. Sexy. A wonderful lover. That he's driving you wild with desire. And mean it! Abandon yourself totally to the joyful task of giving him pleasure; you'll find yourself getting more out of it than he does!

Q: How many minutes of undivided attention per day do *you* need, and how many does your *partner* need? Are both your needs being met?

109

HOT MONOGAMY
Dr. Patricia Love & Jo Robinson

*S*omething that is unique to their relationship is the way that they deliberately use sex as a way to create intimacy. Typically, it works the other way around. Most couples establish a level of emotional intimacy that then leads spontaneously to lovemaking. Cara explained their opposite approach: 'If we're not communicating, in a major way, if we're at odds about money, for example, which can be a major issue, then this chasm grows. We've found that we can use intercourse to forge a connection for us, sex can be the truest form of communication.'

Thomas added, 'To make love this way, you have to get rid of the mental idea that you have to feel a certain way, be turned on, feel close, in order to have sex. You don't. You can just decide to do it. For us, closeness can come as a result of having sex.'

"We've invented a name for this kind of lovemaking," said Cara. "We call it a marital. It doesn't require that we have orgasm, and it's not necessarily very romantic. It can be almost mechanical. But it reestablishes that physical, sexual connection between us, which makes all our other problems seem more manageable."

Q: When you're turned on and your lover's not, how often do you have sex anyway?

110

MY SECRET GARDEN
Nancy Friday

I suggest that the next time you see that pretty female face with the Mona Lisa smile you consider, just consider, that she may not be thinking of a knight on a horse, just the horse.

Q: Should lovers tell each other *all* their sexual fantasies?

111

SEX SECRETS OF THE OTHER WOMAN
Graham Masterton

*I*f you can discover the 'trigger' fantasy that stimulates your man, you can have tremendous control over his sexual arousal. You can enhance his physical excitement by joining in his fantasy, embellishing it, becoming part of it. What you can do, in fact, is to make yourself indistinguishable from his most powerful sexual thoughts.

Q: What is the one fantasy–the *trigger* fantasy–that you think about most?

112

HOW TO DRIVE YOUR MAN WILD IN BED
Graham Masterton

*W*hen you actually have your orgasm, tell him what it's like. Some men seem to believe that it's nothing more than a quiet muscular wince, while others expect the Fourth of July to come bursting out of your ears. Good sex is always founded on good communication between lovers, and if he knows what your orgasm feels like, then he can identify more with your experience when he's making love to you.

Q: Before you climax, *how* do you make sure your lover has been satisfied?

113

ONE HOUR ORGASM
Dr. Bob Schwartz, Ph.D.

*'P*eaking' is a technique that is designed to increase your ability to feel. As you are rubbing yourself and begin to feel the sexual pressure or tumescence build up in you, stop rubbing or slow down, or change direction. Especially do this when you are on the verge of an orgasm. As tumescence builds, bring yourself as close to the upper side of that feeling as is possible without going over the top...then let yourself down by stopping, slowing down, changing to a lighter pressure, or changing the direction you are rubbing.

$Q:$ How many times do you like to be brought to the brink of orgasm before it actually happens?

114

THE GUIDE TO GETTING IT ON
Paul Joannides

*A*nother interesting way of enjoying intercourse without thrusting is to play "squeezing genitals." It is based upon the anatomical fact that when the male squeezes or contracts his erect penis it momentarily changes diameter, and when the woman squeezes her vagina it hugs the penis—sometimes rather snugly and with memorable results. To play "squeezing genitals," partners alternate squeezing their genitals. This can be extremely satisfying if your pelvic muscles are in really good shape, and it doesn't require a particularly high I.Q.

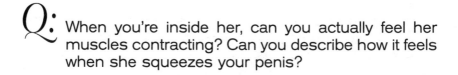

Q: When you're inside her, can you actually feel her muscles contracting? Can you describe how it feels when she squeezes your penis?

115

WHAT MEN REALLY WANT
Susan Crain Bakos

*A*nd many men ask: Why won't she masturbate for me?

"It really gets me going to watch a woman masturbate herself. That is one of the sexiest things a woman can do for a man. Yet few of the women I've been with are willing to do it. I had a lover who would look at me the whole time she rubbed circles around her clitoris. When her hips started grinding and her eyes got heavy, I almost came in my pants. That woman was hot," writes a chemical engineer.

Q: When watching your lover stimulate herself, what goes through your mind?

116

WOMEN ON TOP
Nancy Friday

I hadn't yet learned that for women masturbation without fantasy is rare. It simply hadn't occurred to me that women could be more guilty about what they were thinking than what they were doing.

It is the mind that carries the genesis of sexual life, inhibits us from orgasm or releases us. Masturbation gets its fire, its life from what is sparked in the mind. The fingers might move across the clitoral region indefinitely without orgasm; only when the mind constructs the correct image, a scenario meaningful and powerful to us alone because it carries us up and past all fears of reprisals and into that forbidden interior world that is our own sexual psyche -- only then do we come.

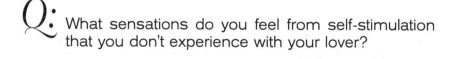

Q: What sensations do you feel from self-stimulation that you don't experience with your lover?

117

MORE WAYS TO DRIVE YOUR MAN WILD IN BED

Graham Masterton

I asked fifty different men from different backgrounds what their greatest sexual fear was and apart from an understandable percentage who were worried that they would not be able to get and keep an erection when they were in bed with a woman whom they wanted to impress, the largest proportion of them admitted that they were anxious about not being able to satisfy their women.

Q: How important is your woman's orgasm to you? How do you feel when she doesn't have one?

118

SECRETS ABOUT MEN EVERY WOMAN SHOULD KNOW
Barbara De Angelis, Ph.D.

"*When* I undress a woman, and notice that she is wearing ugly underwear, it makes me feel three things: One, that she must not care that much about herself if she can actually wear that stuff; two, that she must not care that much about me to let me see her wearing that stuff; and three, that she must not care that much about sex, because she couldn't possibly feel sexy wearing that stuff!"

Q: What's your favorite kind of panties? Which of the following best describes the one kind of panty that your lover usually wears: erotic, sexy, plain and functional, or absolutely nothing?

119

THE GUIDE TO GETTING IT ON
Paul Joannides

Sunsets, Orgasms & Hand Grenades

"*D*efine orgasm? It's somewhere between a hand grenade and a sunset."

- Mr. Billy Rumpanos, lifetime surfer & early supporter of the Goofy Foot Press.

Perhaps it might be helpful to begin with a few comments from Dr. Frieda Tingle, the world's leading expert on sex:

Q. Dr. Tingle, what do you think of "Sex in America'?"
A. I think it would be a good idea.

Q. Do you think Americans are too concerned about orgasms?
A. Whose? Their own or their neighbor's?

Q. We mean in general.
A. Orgasm is very important for many Americans because it tells them when the sexual encounter is over. Most of these people enjoy competitive sports, where some official is forever blowing a whistle or waving a little flag to let them know the event has ended. Without orgasm, they would be fumbling around, never knowing when it was time to suggest a game of Scrabble or a corned-beef sandwich.

Q: If your orgasm had a different sound than it already does now, what would it be?

120

HOT MONOGAMY
Dr. Patricia Love and Jo Robinson

*I*t is quite common for one person in a love relationship to be more focused on sex and the other person to be more focused on intimacy. Too often the person with the high sex drive resists intimacy, and the person with the ability to be emotionally intimate resists sexuality. Clearly this arrangement doesn't work. It's one of those instances when two halves don't make a whole. In order to experience passion, both individuals have to transcend their limitations. The person with the high drive has to become more emotionally available, and the person with intimacy skills has to become more sexually charged.

Q: What kind of compromises do you have to make with your partner in order to be sexually compatible?

121

TOTAL LOVING
By "J"

Silent sex is, if you think about it, rather insulting. If he invited you out to a gourmet dinner, you wouldn't plow through the whole feast without telling him how delicious each course was.

$Q:$ Are silent orgasms as exciting as verbal ones?

122

WHAT MEN WON'T TELL YOU BUT WOMEN NEED TO KNOW
Bob Berkowitz

*A*nd this may come as a surprise, but many times we do not know when you have an orgasm. Some women, of course, scream and yell and make it sound like Mount Vesuvius erupting, and men aren't so numb that they don't know what that means.

But, believe me, there are some women who do not convey the same unmistakable message to a man. I'm not suggesting that you start whooping it up and screeching, 'Touchdown!' every time you have an orgasm. Just understand that many men are unable to break the code. We don't know for sure.

Q: Would you like her to tell you when she is climaxing so you could enjoy the experience with her?

123

HOW TO BE A GREAT LOVER
Lou Paget

*L*ess than 30 percent of all women climax during intercourse! And from what I hear, I think 30 percent is an exaggeration. There is nothing wrong with you. Most women can only climax by clitoral stimulation. We've also been led to believe through movies, books, etc., that simultaneous orgasms happen all the time when two people make love. That's not the case: it is very unusual.

Many times, women get so disappointed and overcome with feelings of inadequacy about not reaching the orgasm they think they should be having, they don't relax and enjoy all the wonderful sensations intercourse does provide. What a waste—intercourse can be heavenly, orgasm or not. But there are ways to improve the odds of having an orgasm. For women, it's a question of learning more about your body and how to focus in on certain areas.

Q: Do you want to know if your lover is *really satisfied* every time you make love—or would you be just as happy to let her pretend some of the time?

124

HOW TO MAKE LOVE SIX NIGHTS A WEEK

Graham Masterton

I have had scores of letters from women who have been married for years and years, and have never experienced a 'real' climax (although they dare not tell their partners).

One of the key secrets to having frequent and satisfying sex is to make sure that you do have regular climaxes...real climaxes, and that your lover is not only aware that you need them but knows how to give them to you.

Q: Meg Ryan set the Gold Standard for fake orgasms in *When Harry Met Sally.* If your lover confessed that she'd been faking it all along, would you be hurt - or would you be inspired to help her find the real thing?

125

THE GUIDE TO GETTING IT ON
Paul Joannides

*P*leasure Toggles. Some men have a spot along the part of the penis that is buried beneath their testicles or all the way back to the rim of their anus which deepens the degree of sensation when pressed upon. Knowing your man's sexual anatomy and keeping a finger on this spot may help move up launch time. (Women who give superb B.J.'s often work these areas with one hand while tending to the end of the penis with their tongue and lips.)

Q: What sexual activity used to make you go "yuck"... but now makes you go "ahhh, yes, oh God, yes, YES!!!"?

126

HOT MONOGAMY
Dr. Patricia Love and Jo Robinson

*T*o restore the electricity to your sense of touch, you may need to be more experimental than you were years ago. Simply kissing your long-term partner may no longer push you over the edge when repetition and familiarity have dulled your senses. To re-experience that backseat-of-the-car eroticism, you may need to step outside your normal routine and introduce some unusual materials into your lovemaking, such as feathers, fur, silk, warm jets of water, whipped cream, warm towels, even ice.

Q: If you had to name one thing your lover does that doesn't turn you on as much as it used to, what would it be?

127

HOW TO MAKE LOVE SIX NIGHTS A WEEK
Graham Masterton

*T*he trouble is, sexual problems are always more difficult to solve than any other kind of personal problems because they're so intimate and because they're all tangled up with embarrassment and pride. Every man likes to believe that he's the best lover in the world, and few women have the nerve to tell them that they're not. Similarly, just as few men have the nerve to tell the women in their lives that their lovemaking is awkward and unresponsive.

Q: How do you *really know* you're good in bed?

128

WILD IN BED TOGETHER
Graham Masterton

"*I* told a close friend of mine that I dressed up like a nurse to turn George on. I think she was pretty shocked, although she tried not to show it. She seemed to think that it was wrong to do something like that to please your husband. But I know for a fact how dull her sex life is; and I also know for a fact that I got just as much satisfaction out of dressing up like that as George did.

"I still put on the uniform occasionally...maybe once a month, once every eight weeks. It's more exciting if you don't overdo it. And that's the only time I shave myself, too, so George always knows that he has something extra to look forward to, when I lift up that little short dress."

Q: What's the wildest outfit a woman has put on just to have sex with you?

129

THE GUIDE TO GETTING IT ON
Paul Joannides

On the surface, men in our society seem more into kink than women. But maybe that's because we define kink differently for men than for women. For instance, a woman who wears her boyfriend's boxers or briefs is at the height of fashion, but if he wears her underwear we consider him to be weird. Our society relishes her kink, but gets very uncomfortable with his.

There are plenty of ether things that are considered kinky when only men do them. For instance, a woman who routinely undresses in front of an open window is thought to be a neighborhood resource. Double that for a woman who plays with herself and/or makes love with the window shades up. But a guy who does these things is considered to be a pervert and may even be locked up.

What a Drag... Some women occasionally dress up like men, to the point of wearing a fake penis (a form of accessorizing known as "packing"). And some men feel a powerful need to dress like women ("transvestitism") Psychologically, a man who cross-dresses might do so to help ease the pain of early humiliations at the hands of a domineering mother or sister figures. Dressing as a woman helps him to feel like one of the power elite, and therefore not so vulnerable. This might be just fine with his wife or girlfriend, in which case all is well. However, problems might arise if he keeps stealing her favorite bra and panties to wear under his suit whenever his law firm assigns him to handle a high-profile case.

Q: What's the *kinkiest* thing you've ever done that still makes you blush?

130

THE GUIDE TO GETTING IT ON
Paul Joannides

*N*ot Helpful. Women who think that their own genitals are dirty or not likable seldom do themselves any favors when it comes to oral sex. For instance, a guy might be having a wonderful time kissing and caressing his partner's genitals when she suddenly pulls him up because she's decided that he surely can't be enjoying something "as gross as that." If a woman fears that her genitals don't taste good, she should ask her partner. And if she feels there is something bad about her genitals, she should tell her partner lest he became seriously annoyed by her rejecting behavior. Perhaps his reassurance will be helpful. (What if he brought her roses and she said "Yuck" or made him return them? It's no different when she thinks her genitals are not worthy of his kisses, assuming he enjoys kissing them.)

Q: *Lots* of things can turn you on. But what turns you *off* faster than anything else?

131

IS THERE SEX AFTER MARRIAGE?

Carol Botwin

*D*on't expect sex to be great every time. Not every sexual experience can be fantastic. Even when two partners are sexually compatible, it is normal for sex sometimes to be good, sometimes so-so, sometimes disappointing—and, with luck, sometimes wonderful. Sexual appetites fluctuate as well. Our hormone levels go up and down; our state of physical or mental well-being changes. These things, as well as events in our lives, can affect our libido. To expect your sex life always to operate at a peak level is to set yourself up for feeling disappointed when normal highs and lows occur.

Q: If you had to pick the worst sexual experience of your life, what would it be?

132

DRIVE HIM WILD
Graham Masterton

"...*Anyway*, we played out this slave fantasy one morning and to my total surprise it was very, very erotic. I think that I got into it even more than he did. I wore a soft green suede jacket and black suede thigh-boots and nothing else at all. God knows what any of my friends would have thought if they had looked through the window and seen me. He was completely naked except for a black studded strap which I buckled between his legs and around his testicles. We laughed a little at first; nervousness, I guess. But then we really got into the spirit of it. I made him get down on his hands and knees and wash the kitchen floor. Then I made him clean the bathrooms and clean the windows and polish all the furniture. Most of the time he had a huge erection, and even when he wasn't fully hard his penis was quite swollen.., it obviously turned him on, and it turned me on, too. I kept coming up to him and flicking him with a thin leather strap, just enough to give him a red mark on his bare bottom. When he was finished I walked around and inspected everything while he had to kneel on the floor. I strapped his thighs for leaving polish-marks on the table. Then I bent over a chair and said, 'As a punishment you have to f**k me.' By that time, both of us were pretty well worked up, and we f**ked like tigers. I can remember screaming. I'd never been so excited in my life."

Q: Outside your current relationship, what single moment stands out as the greatest sexual turn-on of your life?

133

THE SEXUALLY SATISFIED WOMAN
Dr. Ronnie Edell

*Y*our voice is the most versatile sex toy you can add to your collection. Play it for all it's worth! Use it to soothe, seduce, goad, challenge, control, or charmingly condescend and you'll keep your partner on his toes all the way through the final stages of this game. To keep the element of surprise in the tease, use your voice to convey the endless variety of your emotions: intense desire ("Kiss me, now!"); playful disapproval ("You call that a kiss?"); mischief ("Why are you so excited? Why is your penis so erect?"); sensuality ("Mmmm...that's the way I like it."); innocence ("I'd love to touch you there and make you feel really good, but I've never done that before. You'll have to show me how,'); confidence ("Lick me here- and do it like you mean it.")

Q: What sentence do you never, ever get tired of hearing while having sex?

134

HOW TO BE A GREAT LOVER
Lou Paget

*W*hen brushing your teeth, don't forget to brush your tongue and the roof of your mouth. They are the repositories of bad-breath germs and must be swept clean. Brushing these areas will keep your breath fresher for much longer.

Never leave home without mints. When one of you eats spicy or strong foods, such as garlic or onion, you both should eat some. The smell isn't nearly as offensive when you've both consumed the same food, as your chemistries are better matched. And if your lover's breath doesn't smell fresh, take a mint and then offer one to him.

Q: What's your *favorite flavor* of lips?

135

THE SENSUOUS WOMAN
By "J"

*T*he smart woman never forgets the importance of arousing him mentally. Whispering to him exactly what you intend to do to him in bed will create pictures in his mind that are likely to excite him almost as much as the actuality.

Q: During lovemaking, do you prefer love language, lusty language or both?

136

HOW TO MAKE LOVE TO A MAN
Alexandra Penny

*T*he more stimulation that a man experiences, the more intense and dramatic his orgasm will be. The sexually knowledgeable woman will physically prolong a man's erection so that he (as well as she) can experience an orgasm in its ultimate intensity.

Q: Getting there is half the fun: Before your partner touches your penis, what other hot spots she should visit along the way? How long should she spend at each one?

137

SEX SECRETS OF THE OTHER WOMAN
Graham Masterton

$\mathcal{M}$any men feel from time to time that they would like their women to dominate them – sexually, at least. Even the most masculine of men has some submissive aspects in his sexual personality, and can be erotically excited by feeling helpless in the hands of an unforgiving woman. I went to The Hague in Holland to talk with Monique von Cleef, the notorious Dutch dominatrix, whose "house sexual correction" featured such sadomasochistic gadgets as spiked penis muzzles, racks, pillories, and a three-legged milking stool on which her clients would be forced to sit while she told them nursery stories. Protruding from the center of the milking stool's seat was a huge wooden phallus.

Miss von Cleef was quite clear why her business was such a success. Many men in important jobs in industry or public service would feel the need sometimes to be responsible for nobody and nothing, almost to be treated like babies again. They would like to be whipped and tied up. And they would visit her for their "punishment" because they were unable to explain their erotic fantasies to their wives.

"Their wives simply would not understand. They would be horrified. Yet, if they could take the trouble to understand, there would be no need for places like mine."

Q: What's the wildest, most unbelievable sex story you have ever heard from anyone?

138

SEX AND HUMAN LOVING
Masters and Johnson

*D*uring orgasm, penile stimulation is variable: some men slow down, others hold the penis firmly, and others stop all stimulation.

Q: To increase the intensity of your orgasm during intercourse or oral sex, would you like her to speed up, slow down, or stop all stimulation when you start to climax?

139

HOW TO MAKE LOVE TO A MAN
Alexandra Penny

*Y*ou have far more control of your mouth and your hands than you do of your vagina. Your mouth and hands can give your partner a variety of exquisite sensations that can repeatedly bring him to the brink of climax.

Q: What feelings do you get from oral sex that you don't experience during intercourse?

140

DRIVE YOUR WOMAN WILD IN BED
Staci Keith

*R*emember high school? We kissed as though our lives depended on it: extra drool and lots of tongue. WILD tongue. In every orifice we could get to. Kissing is the first form of foreplay. Even by itself, it can be wildly exciting, terrifically sexy.

We used to administer 'wet-willies' in high school too, remember? That was when you inserted your tongue into her ear in some weird kind of simulated intercourse.

Q: What do you remember about your very first kiss?

141

HOW TO MAKE LOVE TO EACH OTHER
Alexandra Penny

Genital kissing, as well as kissing of every other part of the body, is a sensual experience that is meant to give pleasure and warmth to the recipient. Fears of body odors are one of the deterrents to genital kissing. Sex therapists underscore that the natural scents of clean genitals are usually attractants to the opposite sex and that scented bathing or showering can, if desired, be incorporated into lovemaking itself.

Q: For oral sex to be really desirable, do you like your lover's "kitty" to be clean shaven, closely cropped, or aù natural? Do you prefer her to be freshly bathed, natural, earthy, or does it matter?

142

THE HITE REPORT
Shere Hite

*M*ost men were extremely enthusiastic about cunnilingus.

"Oral sex is exquisite. I love every aspect of it—the musky odor—the sweet, think sexy tastes—the textures—the secret ridges, hollows, the crevices—the feeling that I am giving a special pleasure that my hands and penis cannot give. Women's genitals are fascinating—beautiful and erotic."

"I love the way a woman's genitals look when I am close enough to see all of the features. When a woman begins to respond to the act of cunnilingus, her vagina opens like the petals of a flower—her lips fill and enlarge, just as a man's penis does. It tastes like ambrosia that only a woman's body could exude."

"Oral sex is my favorite of all. I feel a great closeness, a deep intimacy burying my face in that dark secret place. I feel that she trusts me fully. I love to look up and see her eyes closed and her face contorted in exquisite agony."

"Cunnilingus is the delight of our lives. I love it. Her vulva is beautiful. I close my eyes and put my cheek against it for a long minute, simply thinking and feeling. Then come long, slow, soft kisses."

Q: What do you enjoy most about kissing a woman's body?

143

THE JOY OF SEX
Alex Comfort, M.D.

*O*ur own experience is that mutual genital kisses are wonderful, but if you are going to orgasm it's usually better to take turns.

Q: Do you think giving and receiving genital kisses should be 50-50 or do you think one lover should give more than the other?

144

HOW TO BE A GREAT LOVER
Lou Paget

*M*ost importantly, I feel, oral sex is the greatest gift of intimacy a woman can bestow upon a man. Between the touch, the sight, and the sound of oral sex, it's almost a sensory overload. Many men have said it's like being in their own erotic film only it isn't an act and they're starring with the women they love. And finally, they are able to reach orgasm without having to physically work at it. For that reason, your giving them oral sex is truly a gift bestowed.

Q: One of the most popular shows on VH-1 is "Pop-Up Video." If your bedroom was featured in an episode of "Pop-Up Sex," what would the bubble above your head say at the very moment when her lips make contact with your *other* head?

145

HOW TO BE A GREAT LOVER
Lou Paget

*K*issing is the beginning middle, and end of incredible lovemaking. For that reason, its power should never be underestimated. If you and your lover are not connected to one another's kisses, there will always be limits to your passion. In order for your sexual spirits to be set free, it is absolutely essential that you kiss and be kissed in a manner that creates heat. An advertising executive from Chicago put it this way: "My boyfriend is a hot, hot kisser. A few minutes of that and I am ready. When he's on top of me and deeply inside, I feel his breath, his hot chest, and we're kissing—I feel loved, lusted for, and safe."

Q: Is the truth of love revealed in your kiss or in your eyes?

146

HOT MONOGAMY
Dr. Patricia Love and Jo Robinson

*W*hen people think about spicing up their love lives, they usually think about trying novel lovemaking positions or making love in unusual places. There's an even more basic way to add variety your lovemaking, and this is to vary the amount of time and effort you put into your sexual encounters. Most couples settle rather quickly into one style of lovemaking. Each time they make love, they spend about the same amount of time and energy.

Quickies have a definite place in a love relationship. They can satisfy the needs of the more highly sexed partner, relieve physical tension, and add more spontaneity - especially when the quickie is a stealthy encounter in an unusual place like the kitchen, a walk-in closet, or the backyard.

Q: What are the three best times to approach your lover for a quickie? What are the worst times?

147

HOW TO BE A GREAT LOVER
Lou Paget

*M*s. Hoover:

How much suction should you use? Due to how our mouths are constructed we can really only suck on the first inch and a half of a man's penis. If a penis is any farther into your mouth, you have to drop your tongue to accommodate it and it is your tongue against the roof of your mouth that creates the suction. Some men have said they prefer less to more suction as the strong constant sucking tends to concentrate all the sensation in the head and doesn't allow for a buildup throughout their entire groin area. Other men love suction and can't get enough. The best way to find out his preference is to ask him to suck on your fingers with the intensity he would prefer and then suck on his fingers to see if you're close. Adjust accordingly.

 Q: "Dear Playboy Advisor: My boyfriend just LOVES when I lick his penis! But what's the difference between good oral sex, and truly incredible oral sex? Any extra tips for an advanced student?"

148

203 WAYS TO DRIVE A MAN WILD IN BED
Olivia St. Claire

*O*ne of the most devastating sexual weapons you have is the odor of your vaginal juices. Men may joke about the smell of fish, but if you keep yourself clean, the musky perfume of your natural lubricant can make an incredible aphrodisiac. The odor of a female "in heat" is meant to attract the male of the species; so use it. Before you see your man, use some of your own *cassolette* as you would your favorite perfume: a touch behind the ears, at the throat, between your breasts, on your wrists. He'll wonder why he can't keep his hands – and his mouth – off you.

Q: What is the aroma of passion?

149

TURN ONS
Lonnie Barbach, Ph.D.

"*I* love you honey." He gazed steadily into her eyes, his lids heavy with sex. "I love you and want to be inside you right now."

She glanced up in surprise. He turned her around and wrapped his arms around her so that her body "spooned" against his, then leaned in close to her ear and whispered, "I want to feel myself inside you. I want to feel you wet and warm around my cock. And then I'm going to move slowly in and out, again and again, for a long, long time so you can come and come and come. I love to watch you come, baby . . ." He groaned with the pleasure of his thoughts..

She felt him grow hard against the small of her back as he gently pressed himself against her. She glanced at the other people standing in line; could anyone tell? No, they were just another couple waiting for the movie.

Q: Women are auditory creatures who get turned on by words. In your best Barry White voice, what would you say to her *right now* to make her legs quiver?

150

HOT SEX
Tracey Cox

*W*hat do men rate as *most essential* in a female sex partner?

- Stamina: 9.1 percent
- Large breasts: 10.3 percent
- Good oral sex technique: 11.9 percent
- Good body: 19.2 percent
- Sense of humor: 20.2 percent
- Being clean: 24.5 percent
- Willing to try anything: 33.3 percent

Q: For sex to be really good, what elements must be present?

151

RED HOT MONOGAMY
Patrick T. Hunt M.D.

*M*ake your lover feel special!!! It's the ultimate aphrodisiac. This is what women and men want more than anything. Everything that follows is, in one way or another, tied in to making the person you love feel wanted, needed, sexy, and desirable. How you make a person feel when they're around you is the key.

And at the end of the day, be enthusiastic about being reunited with your lover. Our bloodhound, Henry, jumps up and down, tail wagging, barking, licking, and drooling all over me. And he does this EVERY time I come home.

Q: What's your all-time favorite aphrodisiac?

152

SINGLE WILD SEXY AND SAFE
Graham Masterton

*O*ral Sex is such an important part of making yourself irresistible to the man you love that you love that you ought to make a point of thinking about doing it at least twice a week-and not just at bedtime, either, What about those times when he's just come out of the shower, and he's sitting around in his bathrobe, watching TV? What about in the middle of the night, when he's asleep? What about waking him, by sucking his cock? What about surprising him in the tub and giving him a licking? In terms of the sexual appreciation and affection that your spontaneous acts of oral sex will earn you from the man you love, you will be making one of the best investments of your life. And that's a promise.

Q: Should oral sex be included *every time* you make love or should it be unpredictable?

153

THE GUIDE TO GETTING IT ON
Paul Joannides

*I*f you offer Dr. Dog a piece of toast fresh from the toaster he couldn't care less. But the minute you are off to answer the phone or are hypnotized by the newspaper's account of how badly your team got beat last night, Dr. Dog grabs the toast from your plate, legal toast has no appeal to his canine senses, but forbidden toast might as well be sirloin steak.

When it comes to sex, we humans are a bit like Dr. Dog. Sex that has an air of danger or forbidden urgency sometimes gets us excited. In fact, sex that's just a bit dirty or nasty can be downright wonderful for no other reason than the element of erotic suspense.

For sex to be as good as stolen toast, some experts claim that it needs to reveal things about you that were previously hidden - little mysteries of the heart and soul. This is easy the first couple of times, since you know so little about each other. But over the long term it takes love and effort to keep sex sexy. It requires that you keep exploring hidden dimensions within yourself and within your partner.

Q: If you could pick the time, place, and sexual act of your next two erotic encounters -- what, when and where would they be?

154

203 WAYS TO DRIVE A MAN WILD IN BED
Olivia St. Claire

*I*magination is the sexiest turn-on of all. So if you want to be an expert lover, you should learn and practice the fine art of mental foreplay. Give him something to think about that will make him hot and bothered, something that will make him crazy to get his hands on you, something that will make him deliciously hard. Sex up his imagination and you'll reap the erotic rewards.

Q: One morning you go to your car and find a small package on the front seat, with a note that says, "Bring this to bed tonight." What do you hope your lover put in the package? What would *you* leave in her car?

155

MORE WAYS TO DRIVE YOUR MAN WILD IN BED

Graham Masterton

*Y*ou deserve much more than a routine sex life. You deserve excitement, arousal, and constant satisfaction. But you will never get it by feeling sorry for yourself and lying back and waiting for your husband or lover to wake up to the fact that he ought to be making love to you better. Whether the dullness of your sex life is your fault or not, you will have to make a positive effort to stir up that man in your life and do for him what another woman would do if she were out to excite him.

Q: If you could change just one thing about the way your partner makes love, what exactly would it be?

156

HOW TO BE A GREAT LOVER
Lou Paget

*M*any women have said that the male-from-behind, or doggie-style, position makes for some of their most erotic sex. Men as well find this position highly charged. Their reasons range from the intense depth of penetration to the feeling of taking or being taken. As a dentist from San Diego said, "It is so animal. I love seeing her butt and seeing me fill her up." Another man, a lawyer from Boston, told me, "There is more smell of sex. I not only feel it, I can smell it."

Q: What sexual positions do you wish that you did more often?

157

HOT AND BOTHERED
Wendy Dennis

*O*ne of the best ways couples have found to inject a sexual thrill into long-term relationships is to treat the encounter as an affair. Here's my favorite success story. He had always dreamed of a nooner. For his fortieth birthday, she asked his secretary to clear his afternoon and she picked him up at the office at twelve. Then she drove him to a tacky motel, where she unpacked a little "whore's kit" of bubble bath, a couple of joints, and various jellies, unguents and motorized devices. After an extended bubble bath a' deux, they leapt on the waterbed and prepared to indulge, at which point he turned to her with a leering look and murmured sweetly, 'Okay, honey, let's put whitecaps on this sucker!'

Q: Of all the wet-and-wild, warm-and-tender, or just plain outrageous sex you have had with your mate, which encounter would you most like to repeat?

158

THE WONDERFUL LITTLE SEX BOOK
William Ashoka Ross

*S*ex and laughter go together. No one knows why. Good sex just naturally brings up bubbling laughter in you. Suddenly you laugh at existence, even at yourself. And it isn't even because anything is particularly funny. You don't laugh the way you would if you were watching a sitcom on TV. You laugh because life seems so simple, so easy. Worries you had only an hour ago are totally gone. All that weight you were carrying has totally disappeared. Isn't it amazing?

Q: What's the funniest thing that's ever happened to you between the sheets—Or anywhere else you've had sex?

159

THE GUIDE TO GETTING IT ON
Paul Joannides

*R*egarding the biology of erections, it is perfectly normal for a hard penis to partly deflate every fifteen minutes or so. Regarding the psychology of erections, be aware that hard-ons have been known to fly South for varying periods of time, from a single day to who knows how long.

The most unhelpful thing a woman can do when a guy can't get it up is to become defensive. Women often assume that erection failures mean the man doesn't find them attractive, or that he might be gay. These are possibilities. But there are about a billion and ten other reasons for not being able to get an erection, from fearing that you won't be good in bed to what just happened on Wall Street. Given the stress of living in the modern world, it's a wonder we men are able to get it up as often as we do. And given the lack of tenderness or excitement in some relationships, an unerect penis might be a signal that the man and woman need to get closer emotionally before anything more can happen sexually.

Q: What is the greatest sexual advantage that woman over men? In the Battle of the Sexes, what is a man's best weapon?

160

REAL MOMENTS FOR LOVERS
Barbara De Angelis, Ph.D.

*L*ooking *into* someone's eyes is not the same as looking at him. When you look at someone, your intention is to stay separate from that person, to view him while your awareness remains in your own space. That is what makes him so uncomfortable — you are seeing him, but he cannot feel you there with him. The distance between you is what might give him the sensation that he is being judged or analyzed.

Looking into your lover's eyes, your intention is that the boundaries between you will temporarily dissolve, and for a moment, your souls will touch. You are looking into him, and opening yourself so he can look into you at the same time. It's as if your eyes are connected to your heart, allowing it to 'see' your beloved. This is what I call the "loving gaze."

Q: When you look deep within your lover's eyes, what do you hope you'll see?

161

THE GUIDE TO GETTING IT ON
Paul Joannides

*I*s It Really Different?

Are men's and women's experiences really different, or do they just use different words to describe them?

Researchers asked men and women to write a paragraph describing their experience of orgasm. A panel of judges cold not tell the women's descriptions of orgasm from the men's. (So much for those charts on orgasm that make men and women look like they come from different planets.) Nonetheless, studies have shown that there are some sex-related differences in the attitudes of men and women, but mostly when they are with members of the same sex. These differences decrease greatly when men and women are in mixed company.

But this isn't what Madison Avenue wants us to think. Advertisers work hard to make us believe that men and women are very, very different. That's because manufacturers can often charge more for products that are targeted to a specific sex, e.g. cigarettes, deodorants, and even hemorrhoid ointments which are for one sex only. It's a little surprising that we haven't seen toilet paper that's made just for a man's or a woman's "special needs" – although one manufacturer, Kleenex, did try to sell man-sized facial tissues, which, by the way, really were better for masturbating into than normal-sized tissue.

Q: What popular advertising slogan best describes your sex life?

162

HOW TO MAKE LOVE ALL THE TIME
Barbara De Angelis, Ph.D.

*S*ecret One:

Sex is very important to men to make them feel wanted. Men take sexual rejection very badly. They feel a woman is saying, 'I don't want you. I don't love you.' Since they don't always know how to express their hurt, they may retaliate by turning off to you, or seeking sex elsewhere.

So if you aren't in the mood for sex with your lover, say no to sex, but yes to loving him. (And men, you should do the same for women.)

Q: She's not really in the mood to have sex, but she doesn't want to hurt your feelings. How could she say 'no' in a loving, original way?

163

THE TEN-SECOND KISS
Ellen Kreldman

*A*n important part of creating a fantasy is being able to alter your appearance to fit the theme of your fantasy. If your fantasy has a camping theme, you wouldn't dress in a three-piece suit or an evening gown. Changing your everyday image to fit the fantasy is part of what makes this special time with your mate magical. Dressing the part helps you become the part, and it's vital to your partner's ability to participate in the fantasy. It's a lot easier to respond as if you really are a patient needing medical attention if your doctor is dressed in a white jacket than it would be if he were wearing pajamas! Can you imagine trying to act out a French-maid fantasy in your flannel nightgown?

Dressing up in a costume isn't just for children or for Halloween. You can have fun experimenting any time of the year.

Q: If your lover pretended to be someone else during lovemaking, who would you want her to be?

164

THE ART OF KISSING
Lou Paget

Secret from Lou's Archives:

*M*en will often watch how a woman eats and drinks to get a sense of how she will kiss and make love. The more robust a woman's appetite, the more likely she'll be open and passionate.

Q: Do you think there might be a connection between the way a woman enjoys food and the way she enjoys sex?

165

HOT MONOGAMY
Dr. Patricia Love & Jo Robinson

*Y*ou can incorporate G spot stimulation into your lovemaking rituals in a wide variety of ways. A woman may find it easier to reach orgasm if her partner stimulates her G spot and clitoris at the same time. ("When my boyfriend does that to me," confessed one young woman, "you have to scrape me off the ceiling") Some women find that lovemaking becomes more pleasurable when the G spot is stimulated prior to intercourse, engorging the tissue and making it more responsive to pressure from the penis. A woman can intensify her orgasms by adding G spot stimulation as she reaches orgasm.

Q: How many ways do you know how to stimulate a woman's G-spot?

166

THE GUIDE TO GETTING IT ON
Paul Joannides

"*I*'ve seen a couple of guys masturbate. I can't believe how rough they are with themselves!" -female

Take this woman's comment to heart. The reason she can't believe how "rough" we guys are with ourselves is because she would never dream of finessing her genitals in the way we do ours.

The best thing you can do when it comes to giving a woman pleasure by hand. Do not even think for a moment about stimulating her clitoris in the same way you do your penis.

With a penis, you can slap it, yank it, and nearly choke it to death, all it does is get hard or harder. Try approaching a clitoris with that kind of careless abandon, and you're likely to be a dead man.

When it comes to touching a woman's clit, assume that softer is better. Always err on the side of tenderness. Push just hard enough to move the skin back and forth over the shaft of the clitoris, assuming you can find the shaft of the clitoris.

Men make a big mistake when they forget to give their fingers a sense of humor. Fingertips that tease and dance will find an especially warm welcome between a woman's legs.

"I like to wait until I can't stand it and beg him to put his fingers inside of me." -female.

Q: Women often complain that they don't get enough finger stimulation. How long do you usually diddle her and what techniques do you use?

167

REAL AGE
Michael Rolzen, M.D.

*H*ave Sex

The more orgasms you have a year, the younger you are. The average American has sex 58 times a year. Increasing the number to 116 through mutually monogamous and safe sex is associated with a RealAge as much as 1.6 years younger (and more sex is possibly associated with a RealAge as much as 8 years younger, depending on frequency and the individual).

Q: How old are you in sex years? And how old would you say the lady in your life is?

168

365 WAYS TO IMPROVE YOUR SEX LIFE
James R. Peterson

*F*or comparison, the top ten sexual activities listed for heterosexual men (in order of preference) are:

- Fellatio by a woman to orgasm;
- Intercourse with a woman in a variety of positions, changing from time to time;
- Nude encounters with two women in a variety of activities changing from time to time;
- Petting the breasts of a woman;
- Anal intercourse with a woman;
- Performing cunnilingus while the woman is performing fellatio (sixty-nine)
- Performing sadomasochistic acts (mild, not severe) upon a woman;
- Being masturbated by a woman;
- Performing simple cunnilingus;
- Masturbation.

The key words, you'll notice, are "a variety of positions, or activities, changing from time to time." Show this list to your lover and find out her particular ranking, then work your way to the top. When you're done, vow not to repeat any of the basics until you've tried every trick in this book. Now is the time for a year of living sexually.

Q: Congratulations! You've been promoted to "Head" Chef at the Grrreat Sex Café. Your first job: Prepare a menu for one entire week of *boinking*, without repeating the same dish twice. What can your one-and-only customer look forward to for the next seven days?

169

HOW TO MAKE LOVE SIX NIGHTS A WEEK
Graham Masterton

*H*aving frequent sex does very much more than release tensions. It raises your self-esteem; it re-establishes your closeness with your partner; it defines your status as a woman; it demonstrates that somebody needs you and desires you.., not just every now and then.., but all the time.

Frequent sex is good for your self-confidence. Frequent sex is good for your physical fitness and general well-being. Frequent sex gives you a more positive and creative attitude toward life and will have a direct beneficial effect on anything that you're trying to achieve, either at home or at work. Frequent sex makes you more calm and less irritable . . . Frequent sex improves your self-image. Frequent sex helps you to explore the full potential of your emotions, your body, and your imagination. Without any exaggeration, frequent sex can change your life from top to bottom.

Q: How often do you have to have sex to consider it frequent?

170

THE GUIDE TO GETTING IT ON
Paul Joannides

*Y*oung girls in our society are raised on fashion magazines that highlight gorgeous female models. As they look through these magazines, American girls often grow up thinking about other women's bodies, particularly the ideal woman whom they hope to someday become. Boys, on the other hand, often grow up fantasizing about doing things, for instance, being firemen, sports heroes, musicians, stuntmen (here in Los Angeles, anyway), eventually stud lovers. In other words, our society wants its girls to be admired for how they look, and its boys for how they perform.

Q: When you were a little boy, what did you want to be when you grew up?

171

THE TEN-SECOND KISS
Ellen Kreidman, Ph.D.

What about me?

*O*n any given day, there is at least one reason to hug your mate. But what if you want a hug? If your mate isn't forthcoming with hugs, then ask for one. If you went through your day and wrote down every time you wanted a hug, you'd probably have a list that looks like this:

15 Reasons to Ask Your Mate for a Hug

1. You're tired.
2. You're scared.
3. You're turned on.
4. You're cold.
5. You're stressed.
6. You've just come home.
7. You're leaving.
8. You're going to bed.
9. You've just awakened.
10. You're proud of yourself.
11. You're in emotional pain.
12. You're in physical pain.
13. You're sick.
14. You feel playful.
15. For no reason at all.

Q: How many times a day do you drop everything you're doing and take time out to kiss and hug your partner? How many times a day do you *think* you should do it?

172

HOW TO BE A GREAT LOVER
Lou Paget

*K*issing is where all sexual synergy starts. When your lips touch- another's, it's the first sign, the first taste, of what is to come. At the same time, despite your mutual attraction to one another, if a kiss feels "off," it's difficult to not feel turned off. A married woman in a seminar told me that she doesn't like the way her husband kisses. I asked, 'Then how can you go beyond that if you don't like to kiss?" She said, "We just don't kiss; we skip that part."

I say, what a shame. Kissing is one of the best ways to get all the juices flowing. But as I listened to countless other women, I began to hear similar stories about their so-called "kissing dissatisfaction." Since then I have heard a number of women and men in my seminars describe their disappointment that kissing is no longer a part of their sexual relationships.

Most of the time, they talk about how passionate their kisses used to be, when they lasted for hours and were the driving force for every sexual encounter. But over time, that passion has slipped away from them, and the kisses slowly decrease in both quantity and intensity. Exactly when the passion began to fade is never quite clear, but most women are at a loss as to how or if it can be regained.

Q: Why does the kissing generally tend to slow down as the relationship progresses? Do you think kissing is vitally important in a relationship?

173

THE GUIDE TO GETTING IT ON
Paul Joannides

*V*isuals. If the man is turned-on by your naked body, for heaven's sake, crank up the lights and park the parts he enjoys most in full view.

Q: What oral sex position excites you physically and visually the most? How much does the position you're in affect how good it feels?

174

HOT AND BOTHERED
Wendy Dennis

*W*hat do men want? No doubt about it, men love B.J.s, Shere Hite found that almost all of the more than 7,000 men she polled were positively effusive about fellatio and gave it two thumbs up. "If I could find the woman who would suck me off in the morning to wake me up," one respondent told her, "I would lay my life in the mud at her feet."

Q: After you've had morning sex, do you walk differently?

175

HOW TO BE A GREAT LOVER
Lou Paget

*I*magine this scenario: dress very slowly for an evening out. Accessorize with a strand of pearls. During dinner, lightly finger or play with your pears. When you return home, disrobe, and remove all but your pears.

Step 1. Begin however you like, perhaps with kissing. When you feel ready, undo your pearls and drag them across your lover's body.

Step 2. Lightly lubricate his penis, then slowly adorn him with your pearls, wrapping the strand around his shaft. Be sure to hold the necklace clasp with one finger as you don't want it to scratch and distract him. Because you've worn them out for dinner the pearls will be softly warm.

Step 3. When his penis looks like it is wearing a Princess Diana choker, start slowly stroking him with a Basket Weaving stroke—up and down with a twist.

Step 4. Then unwrap his penis and, as if you are flossing under his testicles, slowly pull the pearls from one side to the other, slightly lifting his testicles.

Step 5. When you are done, "coil the poiles" at the base of his shaft and settle yourself on top of him.

No doubt pearls will start to have a new place in your heart.

Q: After months of experimenting in the bedroom, you've finally created a brand-new sex recipe that no one has ever tried. It has three secret ingredients. What are they?

176

THE 7 SECRETS OF REALLY GREAT SEX
Graham Masterton

*T*hink of some of the memorably sexy images from the movies—Brigitte Bardot with her blouse knotted, Sophia Loren with her dress torn halfway across her breast, Raquel Welch in her mammoth-shin bikini, Kate Winslet in her wet dress as the Titanic goes down—and you can see that dressing to thrill is not just about clothes but about the way you use those clothes to emphasize your most attractive features and your sexual personality...to focus on your partner's attention on what it is about you that's sexy and stimulating.

Wash the car in a white blouse, making sure that you splash yourself so that your nipples show through. Do your household chores in nothing but a crop-top sweater and a lace thong. Pick your partner up from the station in a severe black turtleneck and black high heels and nothing else. Go to the market in winter in a heavy overcoat and a wool hat and gloves, but remain naked underneath and make sure that your partner knows it.

Q: If you could turn a humdrum domestic chore into a toe-curling erotic act, which one would you choose?

177

203 WAYS TO DRIVE A MAN WILD IN BED
Olivia St. Claire

*F*rench courtesans during the reign of Louis XIV, the Sun King, took great care to create a very special, sensuous environment for their trysts with the nobility. They would sometimes completely redecorate for each different man, including special bedsheets with a design and scent known to please a particular lover. They carefully considered how to stimulate each of a man's senses – beautiful environs with erotic pictures or statues for the eye; sensuous and soothing music for the ear; evocative scents and pungent perfumes for the nose; luscious, juicy fruits and wines to taste; rich, voluptuous fabrics and surfaces to touch. They surrounded their paramours with an aura of irresistible sensuality that brought out each man's sexual best.

Take a cue from these great sexual gourmets and open a whole new world of erotic pleasure for yourself and your man. Remember that the surroundings you create must be those that will arouse his senses, not necessarily just yours.

Q: What is your favorite room in the house?

178

THE TEN-SECOND KISS
Ellen Kreidman, Ph.D.

*F*or seven long days, I watched as our bedroom was used as a home office, a storage area for Barbie dolls and Legos, and a dumping ground for dirty clothes. After the third day of tripping over a laundry basket every time I went to the bathroom, I vowed I was going to make our bedroom into the love nest it was meant to be.

As soon as I had the energy, I began the makeover. Thanks to the Light His Fire tapes, I knew exactly what to do. I started with our bed linens, replacing the low-thread-count polyesters with beautiful satin sheets. Then I replaced the boring white light bulbs with red ones. I placed scented candles around the room to get rid of the smell of dirty laundry. And I bought some romantic CDs to play on our CD player, which I had hidden under a table.

When my husband saw our transformed bedroom for the very first time, he beamed. That night he told me he had begun to worry that our relationship was taking on the same aura as our bedroom—-dull and dingy. Now that our bedroom has brightened up, so has our sex life.

Q: If money was no object and your partner gave you complete creative control, how would you redo your bedroom?

179

SECRETS OF SIZZLIN' SEX
Cricket Richmond & Ginny Valletti

*W*omen erotically aware make room for a chair. They know it's used for more than sitting or plunking clothes on. Space permitting, a chaise lounge is an alluring accessory, since you can position yourself in a variety of pleasurable ways. A Victorian rocker or wicker chair with plump cushions and matching ottoman keeps you sitting pretty. A thick, overstuffed armchair or recliner can elevate eroticism. Almost any chair could be useful for amour and more. What's this, you'd love adding a neat seat but, there's no room? Suspend your derriere in an artsy, woven swing. Requiring no floor space, it can be slipped off the hook when swinging sessions are put to sleep.

Q: What's the sexiest thing you've ever seen in someone's bedroom? How about the strangest?

180

5 MINUTES TO ORGASM
D. Claire Hutchins

*A*merican women are encouraged to be lazy.

By insisting on oral sex or vibrators, women seem to expect the man to be in charge. He must orchestrate the seduction, arouse his partner and keep himself from coming too soon. In the old days, women waited for men to lead sexually, to make initiating moves. Females were passive. We have moved from the days where women were supposed to feel no pleasure at all, even revulsion over the sex act, to later times when women were allowed to feel pleasure, but only as passive recipients of male lust.

Today, female orgasm is often the goal in sexual encounters. We are supposed to be that way – we are told by most sexual "experts." Nowadays, we are advised to depend on the man to give us an orgasm, as if a female's orgasm were a gift that a male could bestow! If we allow men to control our orgasms, are we really that far removed from the role of the passive female?

What happened to women's liberation?

Q: When you have sex with your partner what is the *goal?*

181

SECRETS OF WORLD CLASS LOVERS
Jaid Barrymore

*I*t's time to get your creative juices flowing and pick up that video camera. James Spader and Rob Lowe are hardly the only ones who have discovered the infinite variety of sexy scenarios that can be captured on film. There is a veritable crush of prospective buyers just waiting to get their hot hands on that next piece of video equipment. All you really need to be able to orchestrate your own scintillating productions is a reasonably good video camera, a tripod stand and a minimal amount of lighting equipment, if you don't want to rely on natural lighting. Once you're set up with the required basic equipment, you and your lover get to divide the screen credits. There's director, screenwriter, makeup artist and star performers. So be adventurous. Here is where you really get to act out all of your cinematic fantasies, realize any and all of your dreams, go anywhere your imagination will take you.

Q: If you were allowed to stash a video camera any place in the entire world, where would you put it? And if you were to place one inside your own house, where would you hide it?

182

SECRETS OF WORLD CLASS LOVERS
Jaid Barrymore

*L*et's talk about the language of sex. I've always felt that two of the most erotic words in the vocabulary of sex are voyeurism and exhibitionism; as in watching and performing. I especially like the word voyeur. It sort of slides dangerously out of your mouth and sounds like it might inspire a voyage to some delightfully naughty place to enjoy watching something definitely risqué or even something risky.

Q: If you could watch your lover do something non-sexual, without her being aware of it, what would it be?

183

THE DR. DREW AND ADAM BOOK

Drew Pinsky, M.D., and Adam Corolla

*M*ythbusters

Myth: You're not cheating if you're not having sex with the person.

The truth, according to Dr. Drew is cheating is more in the heart than in the act itself. If you are violating another person's trust, you are cheating.

Q: All over the world, men and women are flirting with strangers in chat rooms on the Internet. Are they cheating on their real-life mates? At what point do you think they go over the line?

184

THE GUIDE TO GETTING IT ON
Paul Joannides

*C*onfucius Says...

Many years ago, a fortune cookie maker by the name of Confucius made the observation "One picture is worth a thousand words." But in those days pictures were often works of art done by master craftsmen. Today, pictures flood our senses in the form of television, movies, billboards and magazines.

Q: What is the sexiest TV commercial you've ever seen?

✿

185

HOW TO BE A GREAT LOVER
Lou Paget

*I*t should never be forgotten that when it comes to romance, there are few tools available to us more powerful than the kiss. For that reason, you must be mindful of every kiss you give and every kiss you receive. Kisses send messages– especially in romance. Being mindful of your kisses simply means to be aware of the language that is spoken at all times and to never allow your lips to speak anything other than the truth. And although kissing, just like loving, comes to us instinctively, both benefit greatly from instruction and practice.

Q: If you had to be amazing at only one thing in bed, what would it be?

186

THE GUIDE TO GETTING IT ON
Paul Joannides

Given how sex fantasies are nearly universal, it's a little surprising that we tend to be embarrassed about them. On the other hand, why bother fantasizing about something that everyone else approves of?

Some people have a single reliable sex fantasy that they go back to time and again. Others have a virtual rolodex of scenes and images that help to get them off. Some people know they're horny because of the sexual fantasies they've been having. For others, horniness is something they feel in their bodies, with very little mental imagery.

The content of sex fantasies varies; some are sweet, kind and silly, others are weird, kinky and bizarre; some are action packed and exciting, others are really boring. Some sex fantasies are populated with current or past lovers, rock'n'roll singers, people in uniforms, movie stars, teachers, priests, family members, total strangers, and even furry friends from another species. Here's just a partial list of the scenarios that people sometimes fantasize about:

Being held or cuddled; doing all kinds of sex acts; sex with more than one partner; having anonymous sex with a highly attractive partner or partners; being forced to have sex; watching or being watched doing heaven only knows what; being adored, desired, spanked, tortured or humiliated; being the one who dominates; watching a partner have sex with someone else.

Q: What's your favorite fantasy to masturbate to? And what's your favorite fantasy when you're making love to your partner?

187

WOMEN WHO LOVE SEX
Gina Ogden, Ph.D.

"*W*hat about being really creative about flooding the senses? If you're clever, you can eroticize just about anything you find in your bureau drawers, even your broom closet. Have you ever had a silk scarf dragged incredibly slowly across your abdomen or a feather duster flicked up and down your back and buttocks until you thought you'd die?"

Wonderful sex does more than melt both body and soul; it brings power, energy, and deep satisfaction to all aspects of our lives.

Q: What are three objects that, when looked at, arouse erotic desire in you?

188

THE HITE REPORT ON MALE SEXUALITY
Shere Hite

"*I*f I do not feel love for a person right from the beginning, I will never feel it. You can work at being loving to someone, but not just plain loving someone."

"I've known both kinds of love. I work at the one in my marriage, but once experienced the immediate flame over which I had no control. I suspect the former is more loving (maybe healthier), but the flame is really love."

"It is the strong feeling you feel for someone right at the beginning, reasons unknown. I have observed couples that worked at their relationship, some successfully and others not. I am glad I don't feel a need to work at my marriage. It just happens along. Basically I think we just happen to like each other, and find only a few things that need much altering."

"I have loved many people; I have been 'in love' with only a couple of people. The people I loved, I still love, feel very close to, and will always love and care for; I would do almost anything I could for them."

Q: What is love? How would you define *too much love*?

189

LIGHT HIS FIRE
Ellen Kreidman

*M*ost men can't resist that vulnerable little girl who resides inside all of us, but I have found that most women who were only children or the oldest in the family have a tough time being playful or using baby talk. If you heard messages such as, "Grow up and act your age," or "Stop being a baby," it may be hard for that little girl to come out. You have to experiment with what feels comfortable for you.

Practice looking adorable in front of a mirror. I know that what I've said here feels foreign to some of you, but I'm convinced that men will react favorably to you if you can make them laugh or appeal to the little boy in them. Remember, inside every man, no matter how strong, how successful, or how powerful he is, is a little boy just waiting for permission to come out and play.

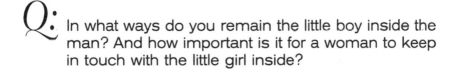

Q: In what ways do you remain the little boy inside the man? And how important is it for a woman to keep in touch with the little girl inside?

190

THE GUIDE TO GETTING IT ON
Paul Joannides

*P*erhaps the missing element in some of the feminist beaver books is an attitude that says, "What we have between our legs is a good thing. It's fun, it's sexy, we like it." Maybe that's the difference between a picture that's clinical and one that's erotic. Of course, some women will claim that men should value sour pusses every bit as much as happy ones. But some of us enjoy knowing that women find their own genitals to be sexy. Perhaps that's why a lot of us nearly ejaculate on the spot if a partner enjoys masturbating and lets us hold her or watch while she's doing it.

Q: If you were a woman, what occupation would you be in?

191

BORN FOR LOVE
Leo Buscaglia

*L*ove Can Only Be Understood in Action

It never occurred to my Mama to define love. She would have laughed at the idea. Everything she did was a kind of loving act. She gave love in our home a tangible feeling. Her love for her children and husband was plainly evident. She was forever looking at us fondly, hugging us (over our false protestations), or sharing in our laughter or tears. She never saw my Papa as a saint, but she treated him as a very likely candidate. You could feel her high level of spiritual love; her every act, thought and deed was an affirmation of the presence God.

Love, for Mama, was not something she thought or talked about. It was something she lived in action. She showed us, as Mother Teresa has, that love is found in sweeping a floor, cleaning a sink, caring for someone ill, or offering a comforting embrace.

Mama, without trying, taught us the greatest, most enduring lesson of our lives; that love is far more than a feeling. It is something to be lived and acted upon, day in and day out.

Q: What did you learn from your mother?

192

HOW TO MAKE LOVE TO THE SAME PERSON FOR THE REST OF YOUR LIVES

Dagmar O'Connor

*T*he last time most couples initiated sex with their clothes on was when they were teenagers—probably in the back seat of a car. Once we are grown up and married, however, we usually "get ready," i.e. take our clothes off, before we even begin. What a shame, especially considering how tantalizing it was to press a hand against a covered breast or, locked in an embrace, to thrust our pelvises forward and rub against one another-with our pants on. "Dry humping" used to drive us wild.

Q: What is the one thing you believed at eighteen that you wish you believed now?

193

THE ONE HOUR ORGASM
Bob Schwartz, Ph.D.

*O*ur job as men is to keep our women happy. Why? Because there is nothing more beautiful in the whole world than a turned-on and happy woman.

Q: When does a woman's face look the most beautiful to you?

194

EMOTIONAL INTELLIGENCE
Daniel Goleman

*C*ontempt comes easily with anger; it is usually expressed not just in the words used, but also in a tone of voice and an angry expression. Its most obvious form, of course, is mockery or insult –"jerk," "bitch," "wimp." But just as hurtful is the body language that coveys contempt, particularly the sneer or curled lip that are the universal facial signals for disgust, or a rolling of the eyes, as if to say, "Oh, brother!"

Contempt's facial signature is a contraction of the "dimpler," the muscle that pulls the corners of the mouth to the side (usually the left) while the eyes roll upward. When one spouse flashes this expression, the other, in a tacit emotional exchange, registers a jump in heart rate of two or three beats per minute. This hidden conversation takes its toll; if a husband shows contempt regularly, Gottman found, his wife will be more prone to a range of health problems, from frequent colds and flus to bladder and yeast infections, as well as gastrointestinal symptoms. And when a wife's face shows disgust, a near cousin of contempt, four or more times within a fifteen-minute conversation, it is a silent sign that the couple is likely to separate within four years.

Q: When does a woman's face look the most unattractive to you?

195

RED HOT MONOGAMY
Patrick T. Hunt M.D.

*W*hat Really Turns A Man On:

1. A woman taking the initiative
2. Perfume
3. Lacy lingerie
4. A women using sexually explicit language while making love

Ladies, taking the initiative with men can also pertain to situations outside the bedroom. Unexpectedly unzipping his pants and giving him oral sex in the car on the way home will always put a smile on your lover's face.

Q: If you could have found out something about sex sooner than you did, what would it be?

196

THE GUIDE TO GETTING IT ON
Paul Joannides

*F*ear of an unwanted hard-on might be one reason why teenage guys instinctively wear their shitis untucked. As for the issue of being aroused by polynomial equations, one woman recently recalled that her first orgasm as a teenager occurred spontaneously during a high school algebra test. She thinks it had more to do with the way she was sitting than the subject matter. She was so astonished and overwhelmed by the flood of sensations that she left the entire test blank, although she was an A-student and well-prepared. She suspects her female teacher understood what was happening, since nothing was ever said and she wasn't marked down. With more experience and self-awareness, this woman's earlier sense of being overwhelmed by her orgasms evolved into feelings of delight and amazement.

Q: Was your first orgasm intentional or accidental? Would you want to know how your lover had her very first orgasm?

197

5 MINUTES TO ORGASM
D. Claire Hutchins

*S*tep One . . . you climb on top!

Why?

The female-on-top gives you control of the action. There isn't anything that automatically makes female-on-top work, except it gives you great freedom of movement. This position may take a little bit more work than many of us are used to, but you are in charge. Too many of us make the mistake of just lying back and expecting the man to do all the work, and then wondering why we don't have the orgasm we want. Sex is a partnership. To make it truly sensational, you must take at least an equal part in the action. For you, it's exciting to be in control for a change and to know you can do anything you want. Have you seen the movie *Something Wilde* with Melanie Griffith? How about *Basic Instinct*? The underlying message of these movies is that . . .

Female superior is for passionate, exciting, even dangerous women; the missionary position is for WIVES.

Q: How could your lover make intercourse more exciting?

198

SECRETS OF SEDUCTION
Brenda Venus

$\mathcal{S}$ex is about having fun and taking risks, so don't be afraid to let go and be creative! After all, how long can you do the old in and out? Get rid of the ordinary. Relax and be willing to make a fool of yourself. I'm not talking whips, chains and handcuffs; if that's your flavor, it's your business. I'm talking about trying something new and inventive for a few passionate moments, put yourself in a state of inspiration. And remember, there's no such thing as can't.

Q: If you could get your lover to try three new sexual activities this month, what would they be?

199

HOT SEX
Tracey Cox

19 - 5 = happy: Count the number of times you and your partner had sex last month, then subtract the number of arguments you had over the same period. A positive number means your relationship is strong. A negative number means you've got a lot more to solve than just this equation!

Get help if you're:

> Arguing about the same things over and over.
>
> Feeling irritable and moody, bored or frustrated.
>
> Finding excuses not to be together and spending less time with each other.
>
> Not having regular sex.
>
> Feeling like you're "beating your head against a brick wall" when you talk to each other.
>
> Feeling more like roommates than lovers.
>
> Considering ending it – or having an affair.

Q: What are the biggest warning signs of a deteriorating relationship?

200

MEN ARE FROM MARS, WOMEN ARE FROM VENUS
John Gray, Ph.D.

*W*hen a woman is stressed she instinctively feels a need to talk about her feelings and all the possible problems that are associated with her feelings. When she begins talking she does not prioritize the significance of any problem. If she is upset, then she is upset about it all, big and small. She is not immediately concerned with finding solutions to her problems but rather seeks relief by expressing herself and being understood. By randomly talking about her problems she becomes less upset. When women talk about problems, men usually resist. A man assumes she is talking with him about her problems because she is holding him responsible. The more problems, the more he feels blamed. He does not realize that she is talking to feel better. A man doesn't know that she will appreciate it if he just listens.

Q: What is the best advice anyone ever gave you about women?

201

CREATING LOVE
John Bradshaw

Spirituality celebrates life and is in awe of higher powers. Some call the Higher Power God. Whatever we call the Higher Power, we believe that there is something or someone greater than ourselves. We are thankful for our life and feel like praising the Higher Power.

Spirituality leads us to service and solitude. We care for our fellows and take action to show it. We have a love for ourselves. We care for our own life. We love others as an expansion of our own life. We understand that by giving we receive. We grasp that by lighting others' candles, we do not lose our own light. The more candles one lights, the more enlightened the world becomes.

Soulfulness leads us to the realization that spirituality is our human destiny. To be fully human is to be fully spiritual. We are spiritual by nature. We are not material beings trying to become spiritual. We are spiritual beings on a human journey. Soul sees the depth of spirituality in everything and in everyone.

$Q:$ If you could have God perform one miracle today, what would it be?

202

LIGHT HIS FIRE
Ellen Kreidman

*A*lthough there are many things in life over which we have no control, all of us are capable of creating memories. Remember, when we are old and gray, and all is said and done, we are left with only our memories. And what we remember best are those events that had special meaning-those crazy, out-of-character experiences-not whether we served mashed potatoes or baked, how the house looked, or what we wore. As someone once said, "You'll never remember the test you failed, but you'll always remember who you were with the night you decided not to study for that test." Start now to create the memories you and your family will cherish in the years to come.

Q: What do you hope you'll experience before you die?

203

1001 MORE WAYS TO BE ROMANTIC
Gregory J.P. Godek

Satin and Lace

*L*adies: If you remember only one thing from this book, remember this: Men love lingerie. Hundreds of men in the Romance Class have confided or complained that having their ladies wear more lingerie is the one thing they want intensely that their women tend to hold back on. (Scan through a Playboy or Penthouse magazine. You'll discover that there are very few naked women in them. They're almost always wearing stockings, garter belts, or lacy/frilly little things.) Take note. Take action.

Q: When looking through Playboy or Penthouse what kind of photograph *always* turns you on?

204

HOT MONOGAMY
Dr. Patricia Love & Jo Robinson

*A*nother way to indulge your sense of sight is to put more effort into the decoration of your bedroom. When you go to bed tonight, look around the room. Do the colors soothe or excite you? Is the bed welcoming? Do you have mood lightning? The right artwork can help create a romantic or erotic mood, and strategically placed mirrors can give you a whole new perspective on your lovemaking. Buying a new bedspread, sheets, or duvet can both enhance your sensual pleasure and declare your lovemaking a major priority in your life.

Q: What four items should everyone have in their bedroom for great sex?

205

LIGHT HIS FIRE
Ellen Kreidman

The Best Kept Secret About Men

A woman who knows that inside every man, no matter how old, how successful, or how powerful, there is a little boy who wants to be loved and to feel as if he's special is a woman who knows a powerful secret. A man wants to know that he matters to you more than anyone else in the world. He wants to matter to you more than your parents, more than your children, more than your friends, and more than your job.

If he could verbalize it a man would say, "Tell me why I make a difference. Tell me why I matter to you. Tell me over and over again. Don't tell me just once. Tell me every day of my life. Keep complimenting me and recognize my strengths. I want to be your knight in shining armor. I want to be your hero."

Men tend to fulfill our expectations of them and to become what they hear continually reinforced. The way to get positive behavior is to reinforce positive behavior constantly. The German author Goethe said: "If you treat a man as he is, he'll stay as he is, but if you treat him as if he were what he ought to be, and he could be, he will become the bigger and better man."

My husband constantly hears what a wonderful husband and father he is, which makes him want to be an even better father and husband.

Q: What are your three greatest accomplishments?

206

SECRETS OF WORLD CLASS LOVERS
Jaid Barrymore

Kinky Quickies

*W*ould you like to know what five magical words I whisper in my lover's ear if I want him to glow like a thousand-watt bulb? I'll bet you would! The words are so easy to remember. They are simply this: "Wanna have a little quickie?" That's right, a quickie. It sounds a lot like cookie, but after the first time you ask your lover this question, he won't have any problem distinguishing between the two. And I guarantee you this: Your lover will be so delighted with your request that he'll fall all over himself in his eagerness to comply.

Q: What are the sexiest words in the English language?

207

TOTAL LOVING
"V"

*I*t's such a lovely way to spend an evening— or afternoon— or morning— or anytime! Isn't it a shame that when so many couples plan their day they consider lovemaking their least important activity? It may be heresy, but if I had to choose between a sensuous interlude of sex and getting the grocery shopping done or attending that obligatory PTA meeting, I'd take the sensuous interlude every time. And so would most of the happy Lifetime Lovers.

In a good love relationship, sex has top priority. It isn't endlessly shuffled aside to "Wait until it's more convenient."

Perhaps the strongest sexual don't of all is: Don't let your sex life fall into the ho hum rut.

Q: There is an incredibly erotic technique that Laura Corn thinks every woman in America should try. It's called *Crawling the Wall*. What is it?

208

THE GUIDE TO GETTING IT ON
Paul Joannides

*S*everal years ago, a singer named Randy Newman wrote a song whose lyrics entreat his lover to take off all of her clothes, except for her hat. If Mr. Newman couldn't enjoy sex unless the woman had a hat on, then we might say he had a hat fetish.

If both people in a relationship enjoy a particular fetish, then acting out the fetish will be a welcome event. But if only one partner is into the fetish, the other partner might feel that she or he is not nearly as important as the fetish itself. For instance, if the woman in the above-mentioned song loves wearing her hat while otherwise naked, then she has found the perfect man. Otherwise, she may start to feel like a human hat rack.

Q: What is the most popular "male fetish" and "female fetish?"

209

THE 7 SECRETS OF REALLY GREAT SEX
Graham Masterton

Secret 4: Dress to Thrill

After the Christmas holidays and Valentine's Day, lingerie stores are regularly inundated with women seeking exchanges or refunds on red garter belts and black basques and purple G-strings .

On the whole, men and women have startlingly different ideas about erotic clothing. Men are aroused by seeing their women dressed up in whorish, vivid colors, in fabrics and styles that make Gypsy Rose Lee look like a model of decency—peephole bras, quarter-cup bras, G-strings with holes in the middle, open-crotch panties, rubber panties, black lace play-suits, and fishnet stockings.

Q: Lingerie catalogues like Frederick's of Hollywood and Trashy Lingerie report a major difference between the types of sexy items purchased by women and men. What do you think is *men's* number-one purchase?

210

THE TEN SECOND KISS
Ellen Kreidman Ph.D.

*J*acqueline and her husband learned how important it was to pay attention to their bedroom. Your bedroom reflects the pulse of your sex life. In Carter and Jacqueline's case, their pulse was weak and irregular.

We spend more time in our bedroom than we do in any other room of our home. It should be a private sanctuary where you and your mate can be alone together, away from the pressures and distractions of the outside world. A bedroom makeover doesn't require a degree in interior design or a lot of money. All you need is the desire to create a private haven where you and your mate can share your sexuality in the safety of each other's arms.

Q: What items should couples *always* ban from the bedroom?

211

1001 WAYS TO BE ROMANTIC
Gregory J.P. Godek

*P*ay Attention to the "Afterglow Effect."

After you've made a romantic gesture, there's a certain "afterglow" that lingers. Your partner appreciates you more, is nicer to you, and is likely to respond in kind. You feel more loved, and bask in the glow of having given something special.

Romance is not an end unto itself. It's about enjoying your life more fully—living passionately in partnership with your lover. The most successful relationships seem to be surrounded by a perpetual "afterglow."

Q: What *one item* should every couple have in their bedroom?

212

1001 WAYS TO BE ROMANTIC (NEW & EXPANDED)
Gregory J.P. Godek

*S*urprise!

It was Valentine's Day, 1989. My boyfriend had invited me to his place for breakfast. I arrived to find the kitchen table in the living room, in front of the fireplace. It was set with flowers, candles, a delicious breakfast and champagne glasses filled with ginger ale. Although this was a wonderfully romantic setting, I began to sense that my boyfriend was somehow uncomfortable. I waited a while, and finally asked him if anything was wrong. He looked at me kind of funny. Then he stood up and told me he had something for me. He reached down, unzipped his pants, and revealed a heart-shaped note with "I love You" written in orange crayon. The note was tied to his you-know-what with a burlap string. No wonder he'd looked uncomfortable! He'd had it tied there all morning. To this day I have that heart tied-with the burlap string-to the trunk of a stuffed elephant he gave me.

- A.L., British Columbia, Canada

Q: What are men putting down their pants in the morning to turn women on in the evening?

213

THE GUIDE TO GETTING IT ON
Paul Joannides

*I*mproving The Way Your Ejaculate Tastes: Some people claim that vegetarians, both male and female, taste better than their carnivore brethren, or maybe this is just propaganda from cows and chickens. At the very least:, red meat is said to make some men taste strongly. Dairy products are said to make ejaculate taste bad, but not nearly as bad as asparagus. Also, smoking and/or drinking coffee might cause a guy's ejaculate to taste strong or bitter. (Perhaps Starbucks can formulate a new blend of beans and call it "Ejaculate Lite." Also, the combination of smoking and coffee drinking make for hideous smelling breath.) A guy might also try holding off on the garlic and pasta sauce to see if it improves the way he tastes.

Q: What foods could a man eat during the day to guarantee he's sweet-tasting at the moment of orgasm?

214

365 WAYS TO IMPROVE YOUR SEX LIFE
James R. Petersen

*S*ay Good-bye to the Same Old Same Old

According to the Association for Research, Inc., the ten sexual activities preferred by heterosexual women (in order of preference) are: "(1) Gentle cunnilingus (on the clitoris) by a man (much emphasis on the gentle); (2) gentle finger stimulation of the clitoris by a man; (3) sexual intercourse on top of a man; (4) sexual intercourse in a variety of changing positions; (5) receiving cunnilingus (gentle, of course) while performing fellatio (sixty-nine); (6) massaging a man all over; (7) masturbating a man; (8) being petted, kissed, and stimulated manually and orally by two men, culminating in intercourse with one man while the other alternates between gently stroking the clitoris and the nipples; (9) masturbation; (10) performing simple fellatio." The key work, in case you missed it, is "gentle." We can see Billboard publishing a weekly chart: "And number 5 with a bullet ..."

Q: In a recent *Glamour* magazine poll of over 10,000 Americans, only *10 percent* of men said they enjoy doing this to a woman's body, but nearly *95 percent* of women said they found this activity extremely arousing. What is it?

215

THE GUIDE TO GETTING IT ON
Paul Joannides

*W*hat Society Finds Erotic

Each culture has its own definition of what's erotic and what isn't. Here are some examples of how these definitions differ from culture to culture year to year:

In Japan, it's a common practice for people to strip naked and bathe together. Nobody finds this kind of public nudity to be erotic or shameful, but Lord help two Japanese who kiss in public. In our society, it's nearly the opposite, with kissing being fine but public nudity being a legal offense.

Q: In ancient times, the Japanese culture had a rule that said after a night of lovemaking, the man had to do something for his lady before she awakened. What was it?

216

THE TOTAL WOMAN
Marabel Morgan

*C*olumnist Ann Landers discovered from a prominent divorce lawyer that nine out of ten divorces start in the bedroom. When a marriage goes on the rocks, the rocks are usually in the mattress. If a couple has a really good sexual relationship, they will try a lot harder to work out their problems and stay married.

Q: In his famous best-seller *Think & Grow Rich* (which has sold over 10 million copies!), author Napoleon Hill interviewed 500 of the most successful men in America on the qualities that created success. Remarkably, all 500 men gave credit to their wives. What made these marriages so unique and extraordinary?

217

BORN FOR LOVE
Leo Buscaglia

Love's Priorities

A successful way to determine how much we truly care for someone is to discern how high their happiness and welfare are on our priority list. This may sound mechanical and arbitrary, but it is a simple and reliable indicator for measuring our love.

We all have personal priorities, whether conscious or not, when it comes to how we apportion our time and the social choices we make. For example, how often do we place our own needs and desires over those of the people we love? Is our lover's desire to attend a dinner party on a specific evening more important than our missing a baseball game, a concert or a night out with the girls or boys? Do we keep loved ones waiting because we consider our time far more valuable than theirs? Just how willing are we to postpone our desires and reorder our priorities for their happiness?

This does not mean that we should be constantly readjusting our lives for the sake of others. It does suggest that we might be more able to judge how much we value our loving relationships by taking an honest look at our behavioral priorities.

Q: Fill-in-the-blank: After twenty years of researching the phenomenon of love, a research project conducted at the University of California concluded that the overwhelming factor in whether or not you will love someone is _____.

218

HOW TO ROMANCE THE WOMAN YOU LOVE THE WAY *SHE* WANTS YOU TO!

Lucy Sanna with Kathy Miller

Our survey made this very clear. In answer to the question "Why isn't he more romantic?" survey respondents told us, "He doesn't know what I want."

But isn't this her fault? After all, if she wants something, why doesn't she just say so? Because it's not romantic, that's why.

Romance is a pretty little drama played out with suspense, intrigue, and surprise. Romance involves working behind the scenes.

Besides, women have been taught that asking for something is rude. If a man cares enough, they say, he'll find out what she wants. In any case, it's much more romantic if it was his idea. Well, that's the way many women think.

Q: Fill-in-the-blank: In order to find out what women want from their sexual partners, the authors of the best-selling book *How To Romance A Woman You Love The Way She Wants You To* asked 5,000 women what makes them feel sexy and desire more sex. The two responses that came up again and again are: _____ and ____.

219

SECRETS OF WORLD CLASS LOVERS
Jaid Barrymore

*R*omance: Women are tremendously drawn to, wooed by and completely captivated by a romantic approach. Something as simple as opening a car door, sending her flowers, mailing her an unexpected love note or surprising her with a favorite perfume is considered by women to be very romantic. Serenading her with a love song, taking her into your arms at unexpected moments and starting to dance while whispering adorations in her ear will coax her into a receptive and responsive mood even if initially that's the last thing on her mind!

Complimenting her on how beautiful she is in the middle of something completely unrelated will always bring a smile of surprise and pleasure to her face. Telling her you love her, even in the middle of an argument, is equally disarming. Having her car washed, doing certain chores without being asked, sneaking off with her at unexpected times and writing her love poems all go under the heading of very romantic.

Now to those men who think that being romantic is a bit too cornball and mushy—think again, because it works almost embarrassingly well! So much so that it's one of the most powerful techniques a man can implement to ignite a woman's passion.

Q: Fill-in-the-blank: Women will write a guy off lickety-split if his _____ are all wrong!

220

THE TEN-SECOND KISS
Ellen Kreidman, Ph.D.

*T*here are twenty-four hours in any given day. Every day of our life begins with 86,400 seconds to do with as we choose. We can either fritter away our time, spending our moments foolishly as if they were just so much loose change, or we can realize that each moment we spend adds up to the net worth of our entire life. How we spend our life is determined by how we spend each moment, and how we spend each precious moment is our choice.

I believe that we can choose to live our lives one of two ways. We can either live our life coming from a fearful place, or we can live our life coming from loving place.

Q: The average American will live to be 75 years old. At the end of our lifetime, we will have spent 14 years doing what?

221

WILD IN BED TOGETHER
Graham Masterton

I cannot overemphasize the importance of a woman's role in staking out the length and breadth of a sexual relationship. Within limits, men are prepared to try almost anything in their search for sexual sensation. Ask any man whether he would like his lover to give him more or less oral sex, more or less anal sex, more or fewer sexual variations. Then ask any woman the same questions, and you will quickly conclude (as I have done, over the years) that, as a rule, it is the woman's inhibitions (or lack of them) that draw a couple's sexual parameters.

Ultimately, it is the woman's enthusiasm for sexual satisfaction that will determine whether or not a couple can reach the very peaks of sexual pleasure. Although the man plays a physically dominant role, the woman (by her response to him) sets the underlying tone, and the longer a relationship continues, the more her feelings about sex will affect their everyday lovemaking.

If a woman is sexually knowledgeable, she will be sexually confident; and if she is sexually confident, she will be able to explore the limits of her own passion without fear, and at her own pace.

Q: Several years ago, researchers interviewed 100,000 women about their love lives. To their surprise, they discovered that almost half of these women were having sex *twice as often* as the other half. They found the women who wanted more sex shared a common activity. What was it?

222

THE GUIDE TO GETTING IT ON
Paul Joannides

*D*ear Dr. Goofy,

     Romance is that mushy stuff that fills Harlequin Novels. It is an entirely feminine construct. Men only become romantic when sheer raw sex is assured. Every time I see those pathetic diamond commercials, I nearly throw up on my television. What I want to know is if any guy has ever been romantic without the possibility of sex hanging in the balance?

Dude,

     Owwie ouch! We hate to think what else your parents taught you about relationships... Do you realize that there is not a single solitary woman in the entire universe who would date you if she knew you submitted this question? Were you abused as a child? We're taking bets that your own penis cringes with fear whenever it sees your cynical hand approaching!

Q: According to John Gray, author of the best-selling book, *Men Are From Mars, Women Are From Venus*, why is romance so important to the lady in your life?

223

SECRETS OF WORLD CLASS LOVERS
Jaid Barrymore

*O*ne of the most empowering, gratifying feelings we can give ourselves is the confidence to know we are able to put our lover "in the mood." And what sinfully delicious fun it can be to explore the myriad of almost endless possibilities we have at our disposal in order to do just that. Usually, I call upon my ability to stimulate one or more of my lover's sensory responses, which I love to do because the rewards are so immediate and so worthwhile.

Q: What could you put in a woman's purse that would turn her on *every time* she opened it?

224

HOT MONOGAMY
Dr. Patricia Love and Jo Robinson

A few days ago I was dragging myself into the house after spending six days conducting back-to-back workshops. It was nine o'clock at night, and I was tired, jet-lagged, and in no mood for romance. The smell of fresh bread drew me in the kitchen. There was my husband, ladling out a bowl of homemade cream of chicken soup, my favorite soup. It had taken my husband all afternoon to make the soup and the bread, and he had timed the bread so it would be ready to take out of the oven five minutes before I was due to walk in the door. I felt instantly revived. We had a late intimate supper, catching up on all the news. As we were heading for bed, I said to him, "Now that was my idea of foreplay." We went to bed and proceeded to make love -- not because I felt obliged to him but because I truly wanted to make love to him. It was yet another example of the power of romance.

Q: Fill-in-the-blank: 93 percent of women are attracted to men who know how to _____.

225

HOW TO DRIVE YOUR WOMAN WILD IN BED
Graham Masterton

*A*fter you have stimulated the clitoris a little, part her outer lips with your tongue (not with your fingers) and probe inside her vulva so that you can open her inner lips. They may be open already, depending on what position she's lying in and how aroused she is, but now you can insert your stiffened tongue into her vagina, and relish the taste of those celebrated juices (although don't expect the juice gates of the Hoover Dam to open, because even in the juiciest of women they won't).

At this point, after a little in-and-outing with your tongue, you can carefully hold the outer lips of her vulva apart, which will have the effect of exposing her vagina and her clitoris much more prominently. Run your tongue tip back up to her clitoris and lick it softly and steadily and keep on licking it softly and steadily until you can sense that she is beginning to feel aroused. Whatever fancy tricks you do with your tongue and your fingers, it is the persistent rhythmic lapping of your tongue tip on her clitoris that will bring her to a climax, so make sure that you don't ignore it for too long.

Q: To pump up her desire during oral foreplay, which five letters of the alphabet should you be tracing with your tongue on her clitoris? And when you want to take her over the edge, what one letter will produce the big "O"?

226

203 WAYS TO DRIVE A MAN WILD IN BED
Olivia St. Claire

*I*f you are bringing your man to climax by hand, you can simply loosen your pressure and stop pumping while he's actually in the throes of orgasm (as recommended earlier), or you can try another method that may extend his orgasm briefly; this depends on the individual fella. Try it and see how your man reacts. Keep up your stroking as he reaches orgasm, but lightly. After he's ejaculated, confine your efforts to his scrotum and "G spot." Light pull on the shaft of his penis (stay away from the head) and massage his scrotum and perineum. This should feel to him as though you're "milking" him for even more juice and more contractions.

There are many delightful ways to arouse your man's penis without touching it, and often this is the most powerful stimulant of all. Suck each of his fingers or toes slowly and provocatively. Thrust your tongue in and out of his ear. Lick his nipples and lift your head as you suck them upward and outward. Let your tongue dart in and out of the crack of his behind; slither it around his anus and underneath to his testicles. Use your fingernails to excite any leftover spots!

Q: There is an item commonly used in a winter sport that can also be used to give a woman a mind-bending orgasm. What is it?

227

THE GUIDE TO GETTING IT ON
Paul Joannides

How Men and Women Experience Visual Pornography

*I*t is often said that women aren't as turned on as men by X-rated movies, and that women aren't as sexually aroused by what they see. However, research is showing that rather than being turned-off by visual pornography, women are mainly turned-off by the premise of most male pornography which portrays females as submissive bimbos. When shown X-rated movies which are smart, fun, and where the sexuality conveys affection, both male and female viewers prove to be highly aroused. (If men were the ones who risked pregnancy during sex, perhaps traditional male porn might have a more caring premise!)

Note: In research on pornography, college students were hooked up to devices that measure blood flow in the genitals. They were then shown X-rated movies. Although these devices indicated that many of the female students were as sexually aroused as the males, several of the women were not consciously aware of their arousal. This may have been due to an experimental glitch. On the other hand, it might reflect how women are often raised to ignore their body's sexual cues. Also it is possible that males wouldn't be nearly as conscious of their own sexual arousal if they didn't have a penis that's difficult to ignore when it gets hard. Whatever the case, women do rent about 40% of X-rated videos, the absolute numbers of which are staggering.

Q: Good Vibrations is one of the biggest company's in the country that specializes in erotica for couples -- meaning that their products appeal to women as much as men. What were their two top-selling adult videos in 1999?

228

WHAT MEN REALLY WANT
Susan Crain Bakos

*S*ex in semipublic places is high on the male wish list. They want to do it on the balcony or patio, in bathrooms or closets at parties, in your childhood bed while visiting Mom and Dad. What's a close second to the fantasy of intercourse on a plane or train, a Forum readers' favorite? Having her perform fellatio while he's driving on an interstate highway. Partly he craves the visual thrill of watching her do something she wouldn't do without being coaxed. And partly the risk of getting caught arouses him.

Q: According to a recent *Redbook* survey, what four types of quickies do women say they enjoy most?

229

WOMEN ON TOP
Nancy Friday

*W*hen we deny our fantasies, we no longer have access to that wonderful interior world that is the essence of our unique sexuality. Which is, of course, the intent of the sex haters, who will stop at nothing, quoting scripture and verse to locate that sensitive area in each of us. Beware of them, my friends, for they are skilled in the selling of guilt. Your mind belongs to you alone. Your fantasies, like the dreams you dream at night, are born out of your own private history, your first years of life as well as what happened yesterday. If they can damn us for our fantasies, they can jail us for the acts we commit in our dreams.

The intent of my friend's rude remarks about my books on sexuality is that I should stop writing them out of shame. In your life, not everyone will embrace your sexuality. Remember envy, especially between women over matters sexual; do not buy their shame and give up your sexuality so that they can rest more easily.

Q: What are the two most popular male and female fantasies according to Nancy Friday's best selling book *Women on Top*?

230

THE GUIDE TO GETTING IT ON
Paul Joannides

*H*and-held shower head: If you don't have one of these gadgets, consider running to your local hardware store to get one. It shouldn't take more than fifteen minutes to install, unless your plumbing is really old and rusty. Hop in the shower with your sweetheart as she tries out the various settings on the shower head. Some women like their partner to hold them from behind while focusing the spray between their legs. This can be combined with rear entry intercourse. Also, keep in mind that when you hold the shower head point blank against the skin it causes the water to bubble somewhat like the jet on a hot tub. This might feel good. Never, never point the jet of water into a woman's vagina as it might force air inside of her body.

(Some men enjoy the feeling of the spray against the side of the scrotum. Depending on how you hold the showerhead, it's a sensation that can be on the cusp between pleasure and pain. This might have something in common with the kind of sexual experiences that some women report, where the line between pleasure and pain is a fine but pleasant one.)

The possibilities for genital stimulation nearly cripple the imagination.

Q: There are countless ways to bring a woman to orgasm. In the book *Tricks* by Jay Wisemen, the author talks about a variety of household items that drive women wild. What are the top three?

231

THE ART OF EXTENDED ORGASM
Kathryn Roberts, M.A

*M*ost of the time most women find the best spot on the clitoris to be between two o'clock and three o'clock. So you just want to rub consistently right in that spot...forever and ever and ever. Some women find just the opposite side in the same place between nine and ten o'clock very pleasurable. But, I would say about eighty percent are going to find it between two and three o'clock.

Q: There's a spot on both a woman's and a man's body that's *not* considered an erogenous zone, but when kissed and nibbled can cause levitation off the bed. Where is it?

232

THE 7 SECRETS OF REALLY GREAT SEX
Graham Masterton

Many men are sexually excited by pain, or at least a limited level of pain. Love bites and back scratches increase the flow of adrenaline, and can make men feel stronger and more sexually energetic. If you find that your love life has become rather mundane, try casting yourself in the role of predatory jungle goddess. Jump on your man and tell him that you love him so much you're going to eat him, and start biting him. Not too hard—there's a very fine line between a bite that arouses and a bite that annoys—but enough to get him aroused. Be playful. Be flirtatious. But occasionally give him a nip that really makes him yelp.

Q: According to Graham Masterton, where is a little-known, highly erotic place to bite your man?

233

ROMANCE 101 LESSONS IN LOVE
Gregory J.P. Godek

*A*re you giving your lover leftovers? Do you give her whatever time is "left over" from the rest of your life? If you don't consciously put her at the top of your priority list, she'll automatically drop to the bottom of the list. It's a Rule of Nature. "People take for granted those who are closet to them." Our culture is not structured in a way that supports love. As a matter of fact, much of society actively resists your efforts to make time for your partner. Your career could easily absorb all of your "free time" if you allowed it to. Your chores and other responsibilities will consume you — if you let them. Here's the secret: You must fight back. You must set boundaries. You must limit the encroachment of the rest of the world into your relationship.

Q: All around the country, people have told Laura Corn time and time again that they know they *should* spice up their love lives but they still *don't* do it. Why not?

234

SECRETS OF SEDUCTION
Brenda Venus

*C*unnilingus is much, much more dependent on your technique than intercourse. During Cunnilingus, a woman's body sensations are quite different than the ones she experiences with your penis inside her vagina – even though they're both nirvana. It's not possible to excel in this art without knowing our lady's intimate anatomy; ergo, the lesson preceding.

Your mouth is a highly mobile organ set in a highly mobile head and therefore provides great sensitivity by the touch of the tongue. It is also vastly superior to your penis. Why? Because if she finds it difficult to orgasm with "Mr. Happy" or if "Mr. Happy" is tired, you will still be a success! A woman can enjoy a series of orgasms of varying intensities before she's completely content.

Q: We all know what *cunnilingus* is. But there's also something called *penilingus*. What is it? (Hint: It does involve oral sex, but what else?)

235

THE GUIDE TO GETTING IT ON
Paul Joannides

*F*ETISH: 1. Reliance on a particular prop, body part or scenario in order to get off sexually. 2. The prop can either be fantasized or exist in actuality. 3. One philosopher has described "fetish" as a hungry person sitting down at a dinner table and feeling full from simply fondling the napkin.

Q: It's time for the Foot Fetish Academy Awards. What wins Sexiest Shoe year after year?

236

HOT MONOGAMY
Dr. Patricia Love & Jo Robinson

*F*inally, sexual athletes can experiment with using the G spot to produce an extended orgasm, one that results in not just multiple but almost continuous orgasms. To create an extended orgasm, stimulate the clitoris until the woman reaches orgasm. Then, as her vagina begins to contract in orgasm, transfer your attention to the G spot. When the contractions subside and the clitoris loses its hypersensitivity, resume clitoral stimulation until she peaks once again. And so on. And so on.

Q: There is a technique called the *blended orgasm* that can give a women two -- yes, that's right, two -- orgasms at the same time. (Lucky Us!) How would you do it?

237

1001 WAYS TO BE ROMANTIC
Gregory J.P. Godek

*R*omantics live in the moment: "Carpe Diem"- seize the day. Don't put it off until tomorrow! Do something passionate for your lover! Do it now! Do it with feeling!

- Do something unexpected for your lover today!
- Do something totally outrageous.
- Do something totally out of character for you.
- Do something sexy. Do something sensitive. Do something creative..

Q: What is the only *sure-fire* aphrodisiac, according to Laura Corn?

HIGH HEEL QUESTIONS/ANSWERS

1. What makes a woman unforgettable?

I originally thought this one was a no-brainer. The three answers I expected to hear most were a woman's breasts, butt, and legs. But my jaw literally hit the floor when I heard the same unexpected answer time and time again: "Her smile." Yep, you read that one right. Guys love a girl with a great grin. As one man put it: "If she has a smile on her face, that means she's loving life. And there's nothing more attractive than a woman's who's happy to be alive."

2. If a woman did a slow, soft, sensuous strip tease for you and left just two things on, what would they be?

Most answers were what you might expect: panties, garter belt, stockings, and a smile. But the big winners were a big surprise. I was especially amazed that most men were so very specific about the type of jewelry they want to see on their dream girl. The top two answers? *Earrings* and *high-heeled shoes*. And that's good news- every girl's got a pair or two of those lying around!

4. What's the most unusual item you've used during lovemaking that really turned you on and rocked your world?

Wow, you guys certainly are creative! Who knew a Scrunchee could be a sex prop? But one guy claims his girlfriend wraps a velvet one around his member when she's giving him a hand-job. Another found an interesting use for a wooden hanger: "I used a silk scarf to tie her hands to the bottom part of the hanger, and then I hooked the hanger over the top of the door. She was so sexy and totally helpless!" Hot! And the number-one answer? Altoids! "When she sucks on an Altoid before giving me a B.J., it makes me feel like there are fireworks going off in my Love Rod!" Stock up, ladies!

13. Congratulations – you're now a member of the fashion police! What's the first thing that should be outlawed on women in public? What should be a felony at home?

That shapeless, oversized baggy look? Men hate it, and can't wait for it to disappear. I suspect that they will never have their second wish granted; we'll continue to wear pantyhose and bras! Around the house? Avoid "ratty old sweats," or a "circus tent, a caftan. I swear, it's like looking at my Mom in her old moo-moo!" So what gets a wink-and-a-smile from the Fashion Police? You'll never get a ticket wearing Daisy Dukes – short cut-off jeans, with a white t-shirt. So simple ... and so sexy!

14. What's your favorite type of kiss?

I think you'll be as surprised as I was by one of these answers. Not by number one, which seemed to be the universal favorite: "Long, deep, French kisses and tickling tongues." But number two is not something we usually associate with men. It's the *surprise kiss*: "When she sneaks up on me and she surprises me with it anywhere, at any time," said so many men. "Those little surprise kisses are definitely the best!" My personal favorite answer? *"The kiss that keeps you home from work."* That says it all.

Dave Barry's Complete Guide To Guys by Dave Barry, © 1995 Random House

The Sensuous Man by "M", © 1971 Lyle Stuart Inc., Carol Publishing Group

What Turns Men On by Brigitte Nioche, © 1989 New American Library, division of Penguin Books USA, Inc.

Sex Secrets of the Other Woman by Graham Masterton, © 1989 New American Library, division of Penguin Books USA, Inc.

Why Men Don't Get Enough Sex and Women Don't Get Enough Love, by Jonathan Krarner, Ph.D. and Diane Dunaway © 1991 Simon & Schuster

Why Men Stray and Why Men Stray by Alexandra Penny, © 1989 Doubleday, division Bantam Doubleday Dell Publishing Group, Inc.

His Needs, Her Needs by Willard F. Harley, Jr., © 1986 Fleming H. Reveli Company

Sex and Human Loving by Masters and Johnson, © 1982, 1985, 1986 Masters & Johnson Institute

Nice Girls Do by Dr. Irene Kassoria, © 1980 Stratford Press

My Secret Garden by Nancy Friday, © 1969 Lyle Stuart, Inc., Carol Publishing Group

What Men Won't Tell You But Women Need To Know by Bob Berkowitz, © 1990 Avon Books

How To Make Love Six Nights A Week by Graham Masterton, © 1991 New American Library, division of Penguin Books USA, Inc.

Is There Sex After Marriage by Carol Botwin, © 1985 Little Brown and Company

How To Make Love To A Man by Alexandra Penny, © 1981 Clark N. Potter, Inc.

The Joy of Sex by Alex Comfort, M.D. © 1974, 1986, 1987 Crown Books

How To Make Love All The Time by Barbara De Angelis, Ph.D. © 1986 Rawson/Macmillan Publishing Co.

The Total Woman by Marabel Morgan © 1971 Fleming H. Revell Company

The Dr. Drew and Adam Book by Adam Carolla, Marshall Fine, and Drew Pinsky, M.D., © 1998 Dell Publishing Company, Inc.

Hot Sex by Tracey Cox, © 1999 Bantam Books, Inc.

Real Age by Michael F. Roizen, © 1999 HarperTrade

The Ten Second Kiss by Ellen Kreidman, Ph.D., © 1998

365 Ways to Improve Your Sex Life by James R. Petersen, © 1996

The 7 Secrets of Really Great Sex by Graham Masterton, © 1999 Mass Market, Penguin USA

Five Minutes to Orgasm by D. Claire Hutchins, © 1998 J P S Publishing

Turn Ons by Lonnie Garfield Barbach, © 1997 NAL/Dutton

Being a Woman by Dr. Toni Grant, © 1988 Avon Books, a Division of The Hearst Corporation

Secrets of Seduction by Brenda Venus, © 1993 Penguin Books USA, Inc., New York

The Wonderful Little Sex Book by William Ashoka Ross, © 1984/1992 Conari Press

1001 Ways To Be Romantic by Gregory J.P. Godek, © 1993 reprinted by permission of Casablanca Press

Mars and Venus In The Bedroom by John Gray Ph.D., © 1995 HarperCollins Publishing, Inc.

Born For Love by Leo Buscaglia, © 1992 Ballantine Books, a division of Random House, Inc.

How To Romance The Woman You Love The Way She Wants You To! by Lucy Sanna with Kathy Miller © 1996, Prima Publishing

In The Mood by Doreen Virtue, Ph.D., © 1994 National Press Books, Inc.

Light Her Fire by Ellen Kreidman, © 1991 Dell Publishing, A Division Of Bantam Doubleday Dell Publishing Group, Inc.

What Your Mother Couldn't Tell You & Your Father Didn't Know by John Gray Ph.D., © 1994 HarperCollins Publishers. Inc.

Light His Fire by Ellen Kreidman, © 1989 Dell Publishing a division of Bantam Doubleday Dell Publishing Group, Inc.

Romance 101 Lessons In Love by Gregory J.P. Godek, © 1993 Casablanca Press

Dave Barry's Guide To Marriage And Or Sex by Dave Barry, © 1987 Rodale Press, and SI. Martin's Press. Inc.

The Lovers' Bedside Companion by Gregory J.P. Godek, © 1994 Casablanca Press

Love Notes For Lovers by Larry James, © 1995 Career Assurance Press and Larry James Relationship Enrichment Love Shops (TM)

Men, Women, And Relationships by John Gray, Ph.D., © 1992 HarperCollins Publishers, Inc.

Real Moments For Lovers by Barbara De Angelis, Ph.D., © 1995 Delacorte Press, a division of Bantam Doubleday Dell Publishing Group, Inc.

The Road Less Traveled by M. Scott Peck, M.D., © 1978 Simon & Schuster, Inc.

Emotional Intelligence by Daniel Goleman © 1994 Bantam Doubleday Dell Publishing Group, Inc.

It Was On Fire When I Lay Down On It by Robert Fulghum, © 1988, 1989 Ivy Books and Ballantine Books, a Division Of Random House & Villard Books

Secrets About Men Every Woman Should Know by Barbara De Angelis, Ph.D., © 1990 Dell Publishing, a Division of Bantam Doubleday Dell Publishing Group, Inc.

The Art Of Kissing by William Cane, © 1991 St. Martin's Press

The Guide To Getting It On by Paul Joannides, © 1996 © 2000 The Goofy Foot Press

PERMISSIONS AND COPYRIGHT ACKNOWLEDGMENTS

The author extends grateful acknowledgment and appreciation to the publishers and authors of the following publications for granting permission to use excerpts from their work in this book.

How To Have Multiple Orgasms by Janice Beck, © 1993 Avon Books, a Division of Hearst Corporation

The Hite Report On Male Sexuality by Shere Hite, © 1981 Random House, Inc.

The Hite Report by Shere Hire, © !976 Macmillan Publishing Company

Mow To Make Love All Night by Barbara Keesling, Ph.D., © 1994 HarperCollins Publishers, Inc..

Wild In Bed Together by Graham Masterton, © 1992 Simon & Schuster, Inc..

Women On Top by Nancy Friday, © 1991 Simon & Schuster, Inc..

Women Who Love Sex by Gina Ogden, Ph.D., © 1994 Pocket Books, a Division of Simon Schuster, Inc..

Total Loving by Joan Garrity, © 1977 Simon & Schuster, Inc.

What Men Really Want by Susan Crain Bakos, © 1990 St. Martin's Press, Inc.

The Good Vibrations Guide To Sex by Cathy Winks and Anne Semans, © 1994 Clies Press

Hot Monogamy by Patricia Love and Jo Robinson, © 1994 Penguin Books USA, Inc.

More Ways To Drive Your Woman Wild In Bed by Graham Masterton, © 1985 Dutton Signet, a Division of Penguin Books USA, Inc.

Single, Wild, Sexy And Safe by Graham Masterton, © 1986 Dutton Signet, a Division of Penguin Books USA, Inc.

How To Make Love To The Same Person For The Rest Of Your Life by Dagmar O'Connor, © 1985 Doubleday, a Division of Bantam Doubleday Dell Publishing Group, Inc.

The Sensuous Woman by "J", © 1969, Published by agreement with Carol Publishing Group

How To Make Love To Each Other by Alexandra Penny, © 1982 The Putnam Publishing Group

Secrets of Sizzlin' Sex by Cricket Richmond and Ginny Valletti, © 1994 Hourglass Press

Drive Your Woman Wild In Bed by Staci Kieth, © 1994 Warner Books, Inc.

The Sexually Satisfied Woman by Dr. Ronnie Edell, © 1994 Penguin Books, USA, Inc.

Red Hot Monogamy by Patrick D. Hunt, M.D., © 1994 CCC Publications

203 Ways To Drive A Man Wild In Bed by Olivia St. Claire, © 1993 In Harmony books, a Division of Crown Publishing Group

The One Hour Orgasm by Bob Schwartz, Ph.D., © 1992 Breakthru Publishing

Tantric Sex by E.J. Gold and Cybele Gold, © 1978/1988 Peak Skill Publishing

Hot And Bothered by Wendy Dennis, ©1992 Dell, a Division of Bantam Doubleday Dell Publishing Group

ADDITIONAL ITEMS BY LAURA CORN

101 Nights of Grrreat Romance
The only romance book filled with 101 detailed seductions, sealed shut until you and your lover tear them free ... and each one a secret until you spring your romantic surprises on each other!

101 Nights of Grrreat Sex
The only sex book filled with 101 detailed seductions, sealed shut until you and your lover tear them free ... and each one a secret until you spring your sensuous surprises on each other!

101 Grrreat Quickies
Never again run out of ideas to keep the sizzle in your relationship. The first and only book with 101 Quickie coupons redeemable on the spot for instant handy-panky.

It All Begins With a Lick ... 52 Invitations to Grrreat Sex
Every week, a hot new invitation. Every week, a wild new seduction. And it all starts when you pull out one of the secret, sealed pages.

The Incredible G Spot Video – *The Ultimate Sexual Experience*
G Spot orgasms. Every woman can have one. Every man can give one. It's not a myth! This video will teach you exactly where the G spot is, and reveal six advanced sexual techniques for experiencing its pleasures. Sophisticated computer graphics based on actual ultrasonic images of human intercourse, clearly illustrated the best positions for stimulating this extraordinary erogenous zone. Live actors show all six methods in a clear, candid and highly sensuous demonstration. And the results? Wait until you hear Laura Corn's guests-both men and women-discuss their reaction to discovering the awesome power of the G spot orgasm for the first time! Must be 21 years of age . Contains full nudity and explicit scenes. 60 minute video.

To order your copies of any of these publications, call

1-800-611-2665

Or visit our Website at www.grreatsex.com.

Laura Corn's Super Sexy Sex Quiz

229. What are the two most popular male and female sex fantasies, according to Nancy Friday's best selling book, Women On Top?

For men, the number one fantasy is a menage-a-trois with two women. Number two for men? They want to be seduced and dominated by a strong, sexy woman.
And this might surprise you: the top fantasies for women are *exactly the same!* They dream of a menage-a-trois with two women . . . and they want to *be* the strong, sexy woman who seduces and dominates a man.

Number one for men is a menage-a-trois with two women.
And number two is a woman in charge-a seduction by a strong dominating woman.
The number one sexual fantasy for a women is also a menage-a-trois with a man and another women. And the second most popular female fantasy is a woman domanting man.
Battle of the Sexes? *What* battle??

230. There are countless ways to bring a woman to orgasm. In the book Tricks by Jay Wisemen, the author talks about a variety of household items that can drive women wild. What are the top three?

Jay Says:
1. Paintbrush 2. Q-Tip and 3. Toothbrush--but not all at the same time!

231. There's a spot on both a woman's and a man's body that's not considered an erogenous zone, but when kissed and nibbled can cause levitation off the bed. What is it?

Corn Says: It's that magical crease where the top of the thigh meets the buttocks. Bet you haven't been there lately!

232. According to Graham Masterson, where is a little-known, highly erotic place to bite your man?

The Master Says: The secret spot is the side of his hip. Since very few guys are used to women biting them there, Graham says that men find the experience highly unusual and arousing.

233. All around the country, people have told me time and time again that they know they should spice up their love lives but they still don't do it. Why?

Corn Says: Because they don't *have to*. They have to go to work, pay the bills, put food on the table but they don't have to romance their partner and so it falls to the bottom of their list of priorities. Sad but true. But it's easy to fix and it's *so* worth the effort!

234. We all know what cunnilingus is. Put there's also something called penilingus. What it is? (Hint: It does involve oral sex, but what else?)

Corn Says:

As the name implies, penilingus starts with fellatio. But then the woman sits on her lover's erection, riding him for minute or two before switching back to oral sex. She continues to alternate until he explodes. Or she gets dizzy.

235. It's time for the Foot Fetish Academy Awards. What wins Sexiest Shoe year after year?

Answer: No, it's not the f##k-me pump. It's the high-heeled sandal. Why? 'Cause foot fetishists love to see "toe cleavage!"

236. There is a technique called the blended orgasm that can give a woman two-yes, that's right, two-orgasms at the same time. (Lucky us!) How would you do it?

Begin by stimulating her G-spot. (You DO know how to do that, right? A little come-hither motion of your finger, about two-and-a-half inches up the front wall of the vagina? Sure you do.) When she's getting close to a climax, *stop* – and switch to finger stimulation of her clitoris. Before she explodes, switch back to the G-Spot, then back to the clit, and then . . . take her over the top with both at the same time.

237. What is the only sure-fire aphrodisiac, according to Laura Corn?

Corn Says: Oysters, mangoes and chocolate may work for some, but good ol' fashioned "variety" is the only thing that works for everyone.

3/3

Super Sexy
SEX QUIZ

2/3

Super Sexy

SEX QUIZ

224. Fill-in-the-blank: 93 percent of women are attracted to men who know how to _____.

Bon Appetit:
Good news--it's oral! 93% are attracted to men who know how to cook. Bonus points if you wear a chef's apron with *nothing* underneath!

225. To pump up her desire during oral foreplay, which five letters of the alphabet should you be tracing with your tongue on her clitoris? And when you want to take her over the edge, what one letter will produce the big "O"?

Corn Says: To keep her kitty in heat, stick with S-T-I-O-Z. As in a "Super Tongue Is Over Zealous!" And to produce the "O", you've gotta produce the "I"--and no dotting, please.

226. There is an item commonly used in a winter sport that can also be used to give a woman a mind-bending orgasm. What is it?

Sexy Stat:
Those hand-warmers you use while snow-skiing can make her hot in more ways than one!

227. Good Vibrations is one of the biggest company's in the country that specializes in erotica for couples--meaning that their products appeal to women as much as men. What were their two top-selling adult videos in 1999?

The second most popular video is really no surprise--it's "Every Woman Has A Fantasy," a years-old erotic classic that sells better now than ever, and it's *very* hot. But number one makes me a little nervous. It's called "Bend Over Boyfriend," and it's about women using toys to perform unspeakable acts on men! Hey, what ever turns you on. . .

228. According to a recent *Redbook* survey, what four types of quickies do women say they enjoy most?

The envelope please...
1. When a man takes charge
2. Right after bathing
3. Nooners
and last but not least...
4. The "Danger of being caught" situation

And remember: Every quickie has the potential of being a longie!

Laura Corn's Super Sexy Sex Quiz

218. Fill-in-the-blank: In order to find out what women want from their sexual partners, the authors of the best-selling book "How To Romance A Woman You Love The Way She Wants You To" asked 5,000 women what makes them feel sexy and desire more sex. The two responses that came up again and again are: _____ and _____.

Sex Stat: The answers are: Surprises and Nonsexual Touching. Why? Surprises make her feel special and appreciated, and nonsexual touching makes her feel truly loved.

219. Fill-in-the-blank: Women will write a guy off lickety-split if his _____ are all wrong.

Strut Stat: It's his shoes. Why? Because a scuffed pair of shoes shows you don't take care of yourself. And if you don't take care of yourself, how are you supposed to take care of a woman?

220. The average American will live to be 75 years old. At the end of our lifetime, we will have spent 14 years doing what?

A: No, it's not having sex. (Darn!) It's watching TV! What's better: Watching *Sex & the City* or *having* sex in the city?

221. Several years ago, researchers interviewed 100,000 women about their love lives. To their surprise, they discovered that almost half of these women were having sex twice as often as the other half. They found the women who wanted more sex shared a common activity. What was it?

Fabio Fact:
They all read romance novels. I've got five words for you: "Book of the Month Club!"

222. According to John Gray, author of the best-selling book, "Men Are From Mars, Women Are From Venus, "why is romance so vitally important to the lady in your life?

John Says:
Because it brings her back to her "feminine side" and makes her feel cherished and well taken care of.

223. What could you put in a woman's purse that would turn her on every time she opened it?

Corn Says: An erotic letter written by you--the juicier the better. If it doesn't make her blush, then it isn't juicy enough.

CAREFULLY REMOVE ME FOR...

THE ANSWERS

84. Do you believe that stopping intercourse just short of orgasm can build anticipation that will lead to a more exciting orgasm at some other time?

Most guys didn't know what the heck I was even talking about here. But the small minority who had actually tried this Tantric technique before really believed in its power. "It's like enjoying an appetizer before the main course," said one. "Trust me, it works!" But most were reluctant to even consider the possibility, however: "It can build to a hernia!, Or what about blue balls?" C'mon guys--it might hurt, *but it hurts so good!*

89. What two things could a woman do to you simultaneously in bed to double your pleasure?

Incredible. Amazing. I could hardly *believe* the wild variety of answers I got. Rather than list the top one or two, I'm just going to run through a rather astonishing assortment of turn-ons: Quite a few guys have sensitive nipples, it turns out; the idea of a woman biting them while riding his shaft was enough to make many a man blush. (One guy mentioned *clothespins* – OUCH!) Lots of men raved about PROSTATE MASSAGE in combination with real sex, with a finger or a toy. Vibrators came up, applied to testicles (gently!) or anus from the female position – think woman on top, facing away from him, toy held between his legs. Hmmm. Sounds nice for *her* too!

Now fasten your seat belt. Each of the following was described with a *smile* by *at least* one man:

* Tightly bound his erection in sheer fabric or women's panties while getting scratched or lightly bitten through the cloth
* Watched his lover's bare bottom in a mirror while receiving oral sex
* Being "ordered" to masturbate in front of his wife while she sucks his toes
* Wrestling his wife into sexual submission in a controlled – and mutually agreed-upon – role-playing scenario.
* Getting oral sex with hot or cold liquid in her mouth
* Making love while one or the other was having an "innocent" conversation on the phone with an unaware friend or relative

Seems like guys have thought a lot about this answer, because most didn't have to think twice before blurting out their wildest fantasies. One bad, bad boy dreamed of having his butt spanked while his lover sucked his love muscle. Another wants his lover to suck his toes while she rides him--all while wearing a cowboy hat. *Ride 'em, cowboy!* Another guy got a bit more specific: "I want her to tie me to a chair, and squat over me so her kitty is just out of reach. Then I want her to beg me to lick it, knowing full well I can't reach it." Talk about tantalizing torture!

120. What compromises you have to make with your partner to be sexually compatible?

One guy said, "What do you mean, I have to give up dating?!" Hah! Smartass. It was the second-place answer that stood out: Oral sex. Universally, men wanted more of it, and were bitterly disappointed in cases where it had diminished. Its meaning goes way beyond orgasm: "It's like she's worshiping it. Totally devoted to making me happy, and there's no better feeling than that." The top answer was definitely not a surprise: Men want more sex, more often, and they want us to initiate it sometimes.

WILD CARD QUESTIONS/ANSWERS

8. *"Blondes have more fun!"* Or do they? What's the difference between blondes, brunettes, and redheads? Of all the women in the world – other than your lover – whose hair would you most like to touch?

We put so much time and effort into making our hair just right, and do you know what men say is the sexiest look of all? "The tousled look – that just-woke-up-from-a-night-of-great-sex kind of wild mane!" So what about styles we might actually wear in public? Long hair got the most votes, but not by a huge margin; there's a substantial minority of men who are passionate about the look of a woman's bare neck. Everyone agreed on this guy's hot compromise: "I love hair that's pinned up . . . and is just begging to be let down by me!"

26. How would you turn a good girl *bad*?

Since guys have been trying to figure this one out for ages, the most popular answer I received was: "When you find out, please let me know!" But more than one man said that alcohol was a great place to start. (Tequila shots were highly recommended when bringing out her wild child.) And I've been told that tearing open sealed-up pages can turn good girls bad as well. So let 'er rip!

42. I think it's fair to say that men have two heads. Which *head* do you follow?

Every man cracked up when asked this question, and every single one admitted they were sometimes helpless to resist the siren song of the lower one. As one guy put it: "It depends on which one's getting kissed!" Another guy said it all when he confessed: "Which head do I follow? Oh, that's easy. I follow the *small* head when it's full, and the *big* head when it's not!" I laughed for five minutes straight after that one!

49. What does sex mean to you?

Okay, this one will shock the heck out of you. If you're anything like I am, you probably think guys look at sex on a purely physical level. It's fun, it feels good, it's the ultimate score. But most of the guy's feelings went much deeper than that. The number one answer I received was not "a good time," or "a physical rush." It was...get ready for this...intimacy. "If a woman lets herself be vulnerable around you, that's the most exciting thing in the world," said one sensitive, great-looking guy. "It means she trusts me and feels comfortable with me, which is the ultimate compliment." The other top answers weren't quite so sensitive. "It means I'm a lucky man!" boomed one guy, while his friend said, "Sex means not having to use my hand as much!" Uh, that's more than we needed to know!

80. Where is the zaniest, most unusual place you would like to make love...but haven't?

For some reason, this question brought out the mischievous little boys in all the men. Since the replies were as varied as the guys I polled, there wasn't an overall favorite. But a few of their dream spots included: "City hall steps, high noon." "On my motorcycle, going down the road on a moonlit night." "In front of all my friends." "Up in a tree." And, last but not least, "On an airplane. It would be fantastic to hit some turbulence while you're joining the Mile High Club." *Now that's what I call flying the friendly skies*

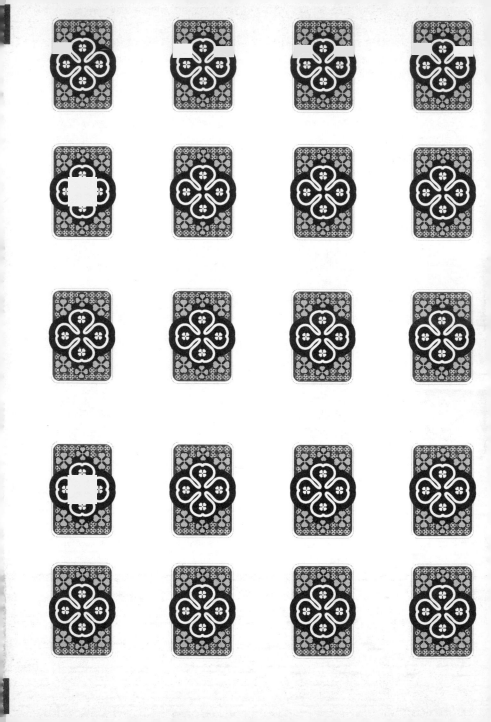

LAURA CORN'S

1/3

Super Sexy
SEX QUIZ

213. What foods could a man eat during the day to guarantee he's sweet-tasting at the moment of orgasm?

Total Tongue-Pleaser: For improving the taste of male ejaculate a man should eat fruit or celery each day. Especially pineapple and apples. The sugar in the fruit gives him a bit of a sweet edge!

214. In a recent Glamour magazine poll of over 10,000 Americans, only 10 percent of men said they enjoy doing this to a woman's body, but nearly 95 percent of women said they found this activity extremely arousing. What is it?

Surprise. It's kissing a woman's neck. You bad boys... it's time to pucker up and do some major *neck-ing!*

215. In ancient times, the Japanese culture had a rule that said after a night of lovemaking, the man had to do something for his lady before she awakened. What was it?

Confucius says:

The man had to compose a romantic poem and have it delivered to his lover before she awakened. Talk about a special delivery!

216. In his famous best-seller "Think & Grow Rich" (which has sold over 10 million copies!) author Napoleon Hill interviewed 500 of the most successful men in America on the qualities that created success. Remarkably, all 500 men gave credit to their wives. What made these marriages so unique and extraordinary?

Answer:

All 500 men had been in monogamous relationships that lasted over 30 years and were still sexually active.

217. Fill-in-the-blank: After twenty years of researching the phenomenon of love, a research project conducted at the University of California concluded that the overwhelming factor in whether or not you will love someone is _____.

Love Fact:

It's knowing that a person loves *you.* It's hard to walk away when you know you're loved.

Laura Corn's Super Sexy Sex Quiz

207. There is an incredibly erotic technique that Laura Corn thinks every woman in America should experience. It's called Crawling the Wall. Can you guess what it is?
Picture this: the man is laying on the floor, with his head about twelve inches from a wall, resting on a pillow. His lover kneels over him, straddling his face, leaning into the wall. She is positioned so that he can flick her clit with his tongue while massaging her G-Spot at the same time with his finger - and it won't be long before she'll be *crawling the wall*, if he does his job right!

208. What do think is the most popular "male fetish" and "female fetish"?
Corn Says: The number one male fetish is sexy shoes. For women, it's the way a man smells. But smelly shoes don't turn anybody on!

209. Lingerie catalogues like Frederick's of Hollywood and Trashy Lingerie report a major difference between the types of sexy items purchased by women and men. What do you think is men's number-one purchase?
Frederick's Fact: The most popular lingerie item purchased by men is the one-piece black lace body stocking. Oo la la!

210. What items should couples always ban from the bedroom?
Corn Says: Any pictures of your kids or family are an immediate libido-buster. Remember, your bedroom should be your getaway--a wonderful space for just the two of you.

211. What one item should every couple have their bedroom?
Corn Says: A headshot of the two of you--clothes on, please--right after you've made love. Every time you walk into the bedroom it will remind you, even subliminally, of the importance of physical intimacy.

212. What are men putting down their pants in the morning to turn women on in the evening?
Sexy Stat: It's baby powder. Whoa, "baby"! According to a famous study, baby powder ranked number two in smells most arousing to women. Number-one was a tie between Good & Plenty candy and cucumbers, but we wouldn't recommend you put those down your pants. (Unless you can't help yourself, that is.)

PLAY ME

YANK ME OPEN FOR

THE ANSWERS

74. **When you've had morning sex, do you walk differently?**

We've all seen enough guys strutting around after sex to know the answer is yes. But are men actually aware they're doing it? The answer is an overwhelming *yes*. "You have a little spring in your step and just feel like the world's a great place," said one. So the next time you have morning sex, take note of his body language. You might be surprised!

176. **If you could turn a humdrum domestic chore into a toe-curling erotic act, which one would you choose?**

Guys really had fun with this one. Their answers ran the gamit from cooking dinner together naked to cleaning the bathroom sink while doing her doggy style. Wow! The most popular response? Dusting. "I'd love to run that feather duster all over her body," said one enraptured fella. Put on that French Maid outfit, and you're good to go!

177. **What is your favorite room in the house?**

If you think it's the bedroom like I did, you're wrong! The heart of the house, according to most of the men I polled, is actually the kitchen. And several men described it in surprisingly erotic terms. "When we're together in the kitchen," said one, "we're tasting things, licking fingers, and bumping into each other. It's foreplay!

81. **If you were allowed to hide a video camera any place in the entire world, where would you put it? And if you hid a Camera inside your own house, where would you stash it?**

Wow, guys really gave this one a lot of thought. The answers ranged from the everyday to the erotic. One stockbroker said, "The Federal Reserve board room. If you knew what those guys were deciding before they announced it, you could make a fortune." What a romantic! Another Peeping Tom-wannabe said, "Are you kidding? The girls locker room over at my old high school!" Yeah, right. Top answer? Any place women get undressed. Think about that the next time you try on an outfit in a dressing room.

As for cameras in the house, answers were more surprising. I thought they'd be more sexual, but, boy, was I wrong! Instead of wanting to watch us masturbate or take a bath, most guys said stuff like: "I want to see what my dog does when I'm gone." Doesn't that shock you? But a few did mention their desire to check out what's going on in the guest room when they have out-of-town guests. That beats watching Spot any day of the week!

182. **If you could watch your lover do something non-sexual without her being aware of it, what would it be?**

This question lit a spark in every single guy's eye. The funniest answer? "Wax my car!" What a romantic. But, surprisingly, the number one answer also involved washing and sudsing. The majority of guys wanted to watch us take a bath or shower. As one fella put it: "Just watching a woman soap up her body--ooooh, that's hot stuff." Better keep that fire extinguisher handy!

155. **If you could change just one thing about the way your partner makes love, what exactly would it be?**

Was your guy shy about answering this one? Most of the men I asked weren't too forthcoming when I posed this question. After some gentle prodding, the answer that came up most was, "I'd want her to tell me what she wants!" Why? One man said, "It would take out the guesswork, and I'd be more confident and relaxed." Other items on the wish list? "She'd want it more," "We'd do it in more exotic places," and "She'd wear sexier lingerie." Girls, are you writing this down?

160. **When you look deep within your lover's eyes, what do you hope you'll see?**

I thought most guys would want to see what a total stud you think they are. But what guys actually hope to see most is the love they feel for *you* reflected back at them. How sweet! And the most amazing response I got? "I hope I see myself getting old with her, that I see my future." I love it!

164. **Is there a connection between the way a woman enjoys food and the way she enjoys sex?**

Most admitted they had never thought about it, but agreed it was true. "There's absolutely a very intimate connection, especially when it comes to oral sex," said one. "After all, you're using the very same senses." One guy confessed, "I'd rather be with a girl with a little meat on her bones than with an anorexic. If she orders dessert and really enjoys it, that means she'll have *me* for dessert later!" Uh, could we see the dessert menu?

169. **How often do you have to have sex to consider it frequent?**

"Um, about every twenty minutes," cracked one guy. I hope he has a very understanding lover! The average number was thankfully much lower--four times a week, to be exact. And most men agreed that frequent sex is the best sex. "If we're having it a lot, that tells me we're a hot couple who can't get enough of each other," said one fella. "And that only makes me want it more." I know it's hard to do, with kids, jobs, and chores--but I've gotta agree with the guys on this one. I really think frequent sex is the Fountain of Youth!

172. **Why does the kissing generally tend to slow down as the relationship progresses?**

Do you think kissing is vitally important in a relationship? When I kept getting the same answer over and over on this first part of this question, I almost fell off my chair. The number one answer? Guys said they "just forget about kissing." But I think the real reason is that the longer we're with someone, the more we let our personal hygeine slip. So keep those toothbrushes handy! The good news: Most agreed that kissing is an important measure of intimacy and a good way to maintain it in relationship. "When you stop communicating and courting one another, you stop kissing intimately," one guy explained. "It's as simple as that." On a happier note, almost every man I interviewed said he was going to go grab his sweetie and kiss her at the earliest opportunity. Pucker up!

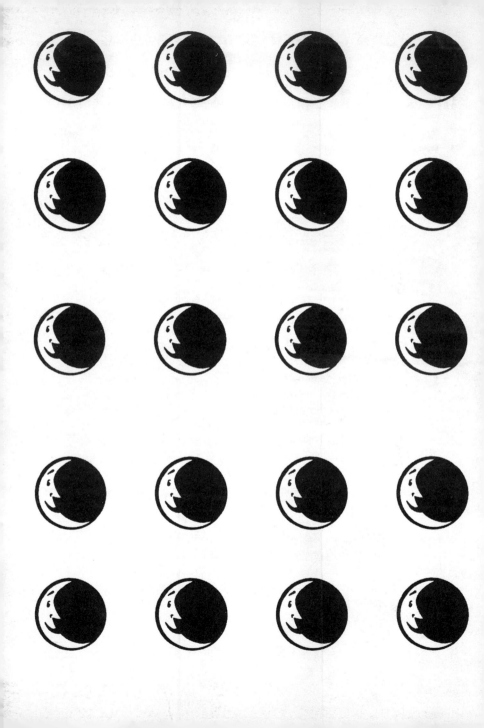

❀DAISY QUESTIONS/ANSWERS

184. What is the sexiest TU commercial you've ever seen?

Did your guy have a good time with this one? Most guys I asked grinned ear to ear when thinking about their favorite commercial, and one came up nine times out of ten: Victoria's Secret. Watching Tyra and Claudia in their bras and panties obviously floats guy's boats. Second place honors go to Polaroid, for the following awesome ad: "It starts with a man in a crowded business meeting," recalled one guy. "He gets a personal call and whispers that he's busy. His wife tells him to look in his briefcase. He opens it up, sees a Polaroid of her, then tells his colleagues he has to leave right away!" I guess it's true--a picture really is worth a thousand words!

185. If you had to be amazing at only one thing in bed, what would it be?

Almost every man wanted to be able make his partner wild with orgasmic pleasure, but the largest number thought that the best way to accomplish that is to last longer: "I'd love to be like the Energizer bunny – just keep going, and going, and going!" Hmm. Is that really what you think women want, guys? The second-place winner was oral sex savvy. One guy said, "I wish I had a tongue like a snake and the confidence of a lion when it came to pleasing her down there!" And the funniest answer? "Being able to convince her that cuddling is a really bad idea!" Dream on!

186. What's your favorite fantasy to masturbate to?

Wow! It turns out there's a BIG difference between the fantasies guys have while making love and the fantasies they have when they're alone. The top answer wasn't a stranger or a movie star, but another woman they know. Startlingly, these sometimes were not women they found attractive in real life, suggesting that masturbation fantasies are often about dominance and power rather than seduction. Hmm. Number-two answer? Multiple women. Surprise, surprise

187. What three objects that, when looked at, arouse erotic desire in you?

Buckle your seatbelts, 'cause this question got every man's attention. They all had unique and interesting ideas, so there was no overall favorite. But here are a few of my favorites: an ankle bracelet, an ice cream cone, a banana, and fishnet stockings. One guy immediately said: "My favorite is a hard nipple pointing through a blouse." Bet he cranks the A/C before his girlfriend comes over!

188. How would you define "too much love"?

A large number of men felt that "there is no such thing as too much love if it's genuine love; you can't ever have too much." But even more were aware of the danger of suffocation. Love doesn't mean "you have to spend every single moment together, explain every second of the day. That's more like obsession." So is personal space compatible with true love? Most said yes: "You can't know how much you miss her if you're never apart!"

TEAR ME OUT FOR . . .

THE ANSWERS

190.   If you were a woman, what occupation would you choose?

I was totally blown away by this response. Men were quick to answer, and they were amazingly specific. Clearly there has been a whole lot of cross-gender fantasizing going on! Some said they'd be exotic dancers, others longed to be housewives. Most of the answers, such as the following, were totally pro-woman: "I would be the leader of the free world," said one guy. "I've always felt that women

193.   When does a woman's face look the most beautiful to you?

If I hadn't heard it myself, I wouldn't have believed it. You might be shocked, too, because it sure goes against the zillion cosmetics ads we see every year. A handful of men said women are most beautiful when pregnant or holding a baby. One true romantic said, "It's the moment she first realizes she's in love." Aw! But the number-one answer by a hundred miles was, "I think a woman's face looks the most beautiful *when she first wakes up in the morning*." Yep, no makeup at all! And answer number two was almost as surprising: "When she's just gotten out of the shower."

194.   When does a woman's face look the most unattractive?

If you guessed it was when she's angry or nagging, guess again! Although those were popular answers, the one that came up the most was: "When she doesn't believe what I'm saying." One man elaborated by saying, "When she has that lack of trust in her eyes and is looking at me like I'm full of b.s., it's like a knife in my stomach." To most guys, jealousy and suspicion are the ugliest emotions of all.

197.   How could your lover make intercourse more exciting?

"Well, for starters," said one guy, "She should stay awake!" Now that's a problem, all right – but I think it's *his*! Sexy lingerie was mentioned most often, followed by sexually aggressive women, then a bewildering variety of specific acts and positions. To me, it was clear that the more serious answers had one thing in common: *men want us to enjoy sex as much as they do*. "I love my wife, but in bed it's like she's letting me have sex, instead of sharing this really hot experience with me." So is a little dramatic acting in order? "No, I don't mean fake it!" said one passionate philosopher. "I mean she should really dig it, really get totally into her own pleasure. Women say men are too selfish; well, I say women should be *more* selfish. Follow what your body wants. Indulge. Show me exactly what feels good. Chase that orgasm. The more you give into the raw pleasure of it, the better I like it. It turns me on to see *you* turned on."

204.   What four items should everyone have in their bedroom for grrreat sex?

"*Another hot woman waiting in the closet!*" said one wiseguy – who lives on Fantasy Island, I think! Most guys were pretty practical: refrigerators and VCRs (with adult videos) came up a lot. Vibrators and massage oil made the top ten. "Pillows, lots and lots of pillows," said one romantic. "Pillows are like Lego blocks for sex. You can build interesting positions." I thought that was *brilliant*. The number one answer? A big, sturdy bed with a substantial headboard, "the kind of thing you could lean on, or really hang onto when the bed starts bouncing. Oh, and of course it has to be quiet. *No squeaking*!" No kidding!

145. Is the truth of love revealed in your kiss or in your eyes?

As a big believer in the power of kisses, I was surprised to find men split right down the middle on this one. "I believe it's in the eyes because then you're looking into the heart and soul of a person," said one Eye Guy. Ah, but on the other hand, a Kiss Believer retorted, "If there's a problem between us, I always know by her kiss. When she's happy with me, we melt together. But when that kiss is distant, it's a ding-ding warning: Relationship Trouble Ahead!" Interestingly, a number of men said the same thing regarding oral sex. We can tell they're losing interest by the they way they kiss our penis--although, as one guy put it, "Even when it's bad, it's still pretty good!" Need he say more?

150. For sex to be really good, what elements must be present?

The top answer will inspire women everywhere, because it's something we can all offer, regardless of age, weight, wealth, or environment. Not that there weren't hundreds of different ideas about what makes up good sex--some of them pretty wild! But there were two prevailing themes. The first had to do with love: "To me, if the passion's there, nothing else matters." Ah, but the number one answer, by far, had much more to do with attitude: "There has to be enthusiasm," exclaimed one sweetie. "Enthusiasm, enthusiasm, enthusiasm! I have to know she's having a good time, or it's a total downer!" So, c'mon, ladies--get out those pom poms and show him how much he rocks your world!

151. What's your all time favorite aphrodisiac?

Ladies, the guys must have been to one too many keggers, because the most popular answer to this one was "Beer," followed by "Thong bikinis." Can you say, "Frat party?" When the conversations got more serious, however, one answer rose to the top: Variety. Nothing kills a guy's sex drive faster than boredom. Except maybe pictures of Marilyn Manson without makeup.

152. Should oral sex be included *every time* you make love or should it be unpredictable?

This one took me by surprise. Roughly half the men wanted it to be unpredictable, and the other half said that it should be a fixture of every lovemaking session. A fan of the latter said, "If we don't have oral, we don't have orgasm. Period." Hmm. Ask your guy what side of the fence he's on, then go from there!

👄 LIPS QUESTIONS/ANSWERS

134. What's your *favorite flavor* of lips?

Men all agreed on one thing: Lipstick tastes terrible! But flavored lip gloss is another story. Strawberry and cherry came up time and time again, as many men said those flavors reminded them of their high school sweethearts. But here's the top answer: "*Nothing* beats the cool, clean taste of freshly brushed teeth."

135. During lovemaking, do you prefer love language, lusty language or both?

Men were once again in full agreement on this one: "When you're with a woman, you want a little bit of both!" One guy said, "I want her to talk like a whore and kiss like a girlfriend." Another went on to say, "You want to know that they love you, but you also want to know that they'll spank you on occasion." Whoa! So tell him you love him, then bend him over your knee and tell him he's been a bad, bad boy!

140. What do you remember most about your very first kiss?

When I asked this, I wasn't sure if most guys would even remember their first kiss. Boy, was I wrong! Most could recite the girl's name, what she smelled like...even what song was playing on the radio. "I'll never forget--it was 'Jessie's Girl!,'" said one guy with a smile. And the thing that men remembered most vividly is the feeling of that first kiss: the heart-racing fear, the sweaty palms, the rush of excitement. Ah, puppy love!

141. For oral sex to be really desirable, do you like your lover's "kitty" to be clean shaven, closely cropped, or au´natural?

Do you prefer her to be freshly bathed, natural, earthy, or does it matter? This one really shocked me. Only *ten percent* said they are into the all-natural look and smell. Twenty percent said they liked a girl to be clean shaven. And an astounding seventy percent preferred a kitty that's freshly bathed and closely cropped. Why? "I don't like to floss when I eat!" cracked one wiseguy. Most said something like this: "You see one that's neatly groomed and trimmed, and you just know that woman seriously enjoys sex."

142. What do you enjoy most about kissing a woman's body?

I expected men to talk about the way our nipples harden, or the feel of our skin. So I was totally surprised when more than 9 out of 10 guys said the exact same thing: "The response I get while I'm doing it." Ooh, I like that! "When my girlfriend arches her head back and moans deeply, I know whatever I'm doing is working." That is *definitely* a good sign!

143. Do you think giving and receiving genital kisses should be 50-50 or do you think one lover should give more than the other?

Think guys would get B.J.s all day long and never reciprocate if they could? A few did say that, but "50-50," was overwhelmingly the most popular answer. Most guys proclaimed, "I'm an equal opportunist! If I get a tongue bath, then so does she!" Yeah! One diplomat did say, "I like B.J.s more than she likes oral, so I get more of it. But I make it up by kissing her breasts, which absolutely drives her wild." Ah, the art of compromise!

this scream like an animal and just exploded on my face. Man, for a week you couldn't wipe the smile off my face!!" Hers, too, I bet!

123. Do you want to know if your lover is really satisfied every time you make love--or would you be just as happy to let her pretend some of the time?

Wow--most guys really do believe that honesty is the best policy. In fact, an overwhelming eighty-five percent said they wouldn't want to be lied to. "I would rather hear a 'catch-me-next-time' comment than to hear the fake moaning and groaning," explained one. A small minority were comfortable with a little white lie: "If I think she's having an orgasm, it will make my own orgasm more intense, so what I don't know won't hurt me." And I had to laugh when one guy shrugged and said: "Why the hell would she want to pretend? You don't see guys faking it, do you? We aren't stopping til we get our orgasm. And girls should be the same way!" Yeah, equal rights!

125. What sexual activity used to make you go "yuck".... but now makes you go "ahhh, yes, oh God, yes, YES!!!"?

Was your guy stumped on this one? Most of the guys I interviewed sure were. After a lot of thought, a few brave souls confessed they were now into being totally and completely dominated--and sometimes even humiliated--by their partner. Other guys admitted they were into nipple clamps or anal beads. But one answer popped up more than the rest: The Prostrate Trick. "You know--she puts her well lubricated finger, uh, up where the sun doesn't shine while going down on you," explained one. "At first, it freaked me out, but now it makes me come like a cannon." Guys have had fantasies about that forever, but now it doesn't seem to threaten their sexuality as much. Let sexual freedom ring!

126. If you had to name one thing your lover does that doesn't turn you on as much as it used to, what would it be?

This question is so personal, I got a million different answers! But one that came up quite a few times was "the sounds she makes during sex." News flash: Our moans and groans aren't always music to guys' ears. "When I first started dating my girlfriend, all her 'oohs' and 'aahs' turned me on," said several fellas. "But the more I got to know her, the more it started sounding fake to me." Other guys mentioned doing it in the missionary position ("Yawn!"), role-playing, and sucking his ear lobes. The lesson here? Don't do the fake thing with your voice and remember just because he used to like it doesn't necessarily mean he still does!

127. How do you "really know" you're good in bed?

While a few guys claimed to "just know," most fellas depended on their partner's opinion in this department. "If she says I'm good, then I know I'm good!" said one smoldering sweetie. Frequency of orgasms was another effective way to monitor your studliness. And one jokester claimed the only way to know for sure is to ask your Magic 8 Ball and see what comes up. Real scientific!

133. What sentence do you never, ever get tired of hearing while having sex?

"Wouldn't it be fun if I got my sister over here right now?" Okay, maybe not! After the obvious jokes, most men agreed that there was one thing they always, always love to hear: "Keep doing that and you're going to make me come!" The most thrilling ten words in the entire English language!

112. **Before you climax, *how* do you make sure your lover has been satisfied?**

This question stumped a lot of guys. "How do I make sure the woman's been satisfied?" asked one wiseguy. "Well, if I've got her Lee Press-On Nails stuck in my back, I figure I'm doing okay." Yes, I'd call that a positive sign! Unfortunately, more than a few said they haven't figured this one out yet. But the majority of men were right on the money when they said the following three little words: "I ask her."

113. **How many times do you like to be brought to the brink of orgasm before it actually happens?**

Good news, ladies: Once you learn his answer to this question, he'll be at your mercy. Most men said *three* is the magic number: "Once she takes me there and back three times, I'm ready to explode!" Duck and cover! The second most-popular answer was: "As many times as possible!" "The more she does it, the more my anticipation builds and the more excited I get. And the more excited I get, the bigger my orgasm is when it actually does happen!" Once you master this technique, he'll totally be at your mercy!

115. **When watching your lover stimulate herself, what goes through your mind?**

I knew this question would be hot – but even I was blown away by the impact it had on these guys. Every single man had a reaction that was as much physical as emotional. Not one failed to gasp or moan or blush very deeply before he answered. "God, it's like . . . every fantasy I've ever had, come to life." The power of this erotic vision went deep, much deeper than mere sex. "She's showing me the most incredibly intimate side of her. It's like the highest honor ever, like she's showing me the greatest secret on Earth." Ladies, it seems that we have some magic at our fingertips: "I'm completely hypnotized by it. The sight of her fingers flying up and down, all that glistening wetness, and that look on her face – she's so completely in the moment, in the sheer raw erotic damn pleasure of it, that I'm swept up in it, too, like she's cast a spell on me." There's a powerful lesson here, ladies; no other question left these men so aroused.

117. **How important is your woman's orgasm to you? How do you feel when she doesn't have one?**

We're in luck, ladies. How important is our orgasm? It's *everything!* An overwhelming ninety percent echoed this guy's opinion: "My pleasure comes from giving her pleasure. If she doesn't climax, I haven't done my job." Smart man! The remaining ten percent who said they didn't care if we come or not probably isn't getting much action anyway! And, with that attitude, they really don't deserve to!

122. **Would you like her to tell you when she is climaxing so you could enjoy the experience with her?**

The answer across the board was an overwhelming "Yes." All agreed that we should know how to give guys the sign that we've hit the big "O" -- it's an incredible turn-on for them. "She used to fake it," said one man, "And I *knew* she was, even though she wouldn't admit it. Pretty good, too, but I wasn't sold, and I felt really bad about it. Then one day I hit the jackpot. The right position, the right trick, and I felt it coming on, and I could tell she was, like, shocked to be feeling so out of control. This deep, raspy moan came out of her, and a few words I had never heard her use, then it started. God, this trembling in her belly, her thighs shaking; she let out

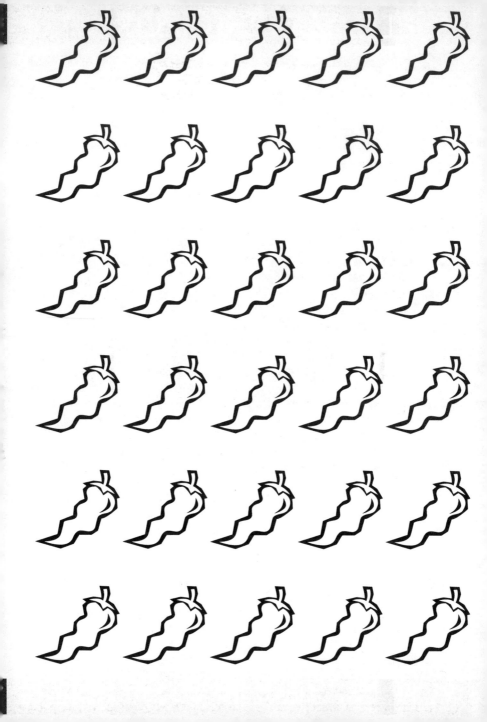

PEEK INSIDE FOR . . .

THE ANSWERS

question. Most guys said that this is the key to a good relationship: "The secret to romance is making sure that the other person in your relationship feels needed." And many admitted that their relationships ran into real trouble when they started to feel useless. One guy confessed, "When she failed to express appreciation for the help I gave her, it was over." So, ladies, let him know how much you need him, and how much you love everything he does for you...every single day!

102. When 100,000 men were asked "Have you ever had an extramarital affair?" during a recent survey, a whopping seventy-eight percent said yes! Why do you think so many men have a hard time being monogamous?

Most of the men immediately fell back on that creaky old "our-genes-make-us-do-it" argument. But this answer rang true with me: "I can tell when she's not into me anymore. Sex gets boring. She's, um, not really into it." In other words, men get their rush from making us happy . . . and if they're doing it right, we should let them know.

103. If your lover asked you to take a sexy photograph of her – one for your eyes only – what would it look like?

Wow – grab your cameras, 'cause guys all across America are dying to take some steamy shots! The favorite pose? "I'd love one of her on all fours, so I could see her beautiful butt!" Almost as many men were fans of the classic beaver shot: "I'd give anything to take one of her on the bed, spread eagle, with a garter belt and stockings on. I get hard just thinking about it!" Most of them said they wanted to see us playing with ourselves, or using a sex toy. Just make sure you use a Polaroid – because no FotoMat is going to develop those kind of pictures!

104. When you're out with a woman, do you only have eyes for her?

Do you expect her to only have eyes for you? Uh-oh! The old Double Standard raises its ugly head here! Most men absolutely did not want their ladies to check out other guys. But, in the same breath, fifty percent said they just can't help but feast their eyes upon other women: "Women dress to attract, so men look. Yes, I have to admit, I'm Mr. Swivel Head when I'm out." Okay, guys, no fair!!!

105. Under what circumstances, if any, could you forgive infidelity and continue the relationship?

Did your man react strongly to this question? Most guys I polled had very strong opinions when it came to infidelity. A whopping seventy percent said they would not forgive under any circumstances: "The minute they cheat, the relationship is dead. It's over." A minority were a tad more forgiving, such as the man who said, "I would hope that if my love is so deep for someone, I would realize that mistakes do sometimes happen and forgive her." Unfortunately that's sometimes easier said than done.

111. What is the one fantasy--the *trigger* fantasy--that you think about most?

No surprise here. The biggie among guys was the good 'ol "menage-a-trois" with two women. Don't they ever get tired of that one? The second most popular sexual fantasy was having the woman take charge--with a little light bondage thrown in the mix. Other popular fantasies: "Sex with an older women." "The stranger in the bar." "Orgies." And, my personal favorite: "The cheerleader fantasy--for guys who couldn't get the cheerleaders to look twice at them in high school." Go team!

91. What is it about love that makes you most afraid?

How's this for a shocker? Two answers kept coming up time and time again, and surprisingly, they're almost total opposites. About half the men said nothing about love scares them, except for maybe a lack of it. Totally fearless! But the other half said they were most afraid of letting us down: "Sometimes nothing I do makes her happy. And all I want is for her to be happy." How sweet is that?

97. Would an unsatisfying sex life without hope of improvement cause you to dissolve a relationship?

How long could you go without sexual intercourse and still preserve a healthy relationship? When I asked the first part of this question, guys had very definite views – and weren't afraid to voice them. Most said they absolutely could not have a relationship with a woman who wasn't into sex. One guy put it this way: "What man wants to sleep next to a woman who doesn't get turned on by him? It's an insult." Ladies, would you want to sleep next to a man who didn't get turned on by you? Of course not! But when I asked guys the second part of the question, I was totally astonished. Most men said they could abstain for anywhere from two weeks to two months before it put a real strain on things. "After about a month of non-action, you start going, 'Whoa, just a second, I'm not feeling as close to you as I'd like to,'" said one. "You can't feel as close if you're not having sex – period." Well said.

98. Do you sometimes like to make love without it leading to sexual intercourse?

Most of the men I talked to absolutely loved this question. I was a bit surprised to find an overwhelming number said yes to this one. Why do they like it? "Because it forces you to be more creative," said one. Several guys said, "This just adds a little more variety! And variety is the spice of life." But one naysayer replied, "If you're not having sex, you're not making love... so my answer is NO NO NO NO NO!" C'mon - tell us how you really feel!

99. If your lover couldn't have an orgasm without the help of a sex toy, how would that make you feel?

Most guys said that sex toys are fine--once in a while. But if you pull out the vibrator every single time you have sex, the novelty wears off fast. "If she can't get off without her vibrator, that means I can't satisfy her," most guys explained. "And if I can't get her off, that's a total turn-off." Other men worried that if she gets too used to her vibrator, no tongue or finger could ever duplicate that sensation: "I can't compete with something that has batteries, bottom line!" The lesson? Use that vibrator sparingly.

100. What makes a woman truly sensuous?

Since this question is so broad, the answers were all across the board. The most popular response was, "An appetite for sex." If a woman likes to get it on, she apparently oozes sensuality. Other favorites? "Big lips," "Sexy clothes," "Long hair," and "A raspy voice." One funny man even said, "The fact she'll have sex with me!" But one guy put it best when he said, "It's hard to describe, but it's not something that can be learned. She's born with it." So that's why they never offered Sensuality 101 in school!

101. How important is it for you to feel needed?

Who says men don't like to talk about their feelings? They all had something to say about this

60. **What's the best thing anyone's ever said to you right after making love? And what's the one comment you'd most like to forget?**

Boy, what a memory guys have! Seems like they remember everything we say after sex--the good, bad, and the ugly. The sentences they'd love to hear over and over again? "You're the only man I've ever had an orgasm with!" ranked number-one, followed by, "You're the best lover I'd ever been with!" Now get ready to cringe, 'cause the worst comments are beyond harsh. The most loathed remark by a landslide was: "Is it in yet?" Ouch! "Uh-oh, I think my boyfriend's home!" was another one that sent guys screaming. And, from the Jerry Springer files, one guy swore he's heard: "Can you believe I used to be a guy?" Scary!!

67. **What is the highest compliment you can pay your lover?**

Most men felt that the highest compliment you could pay someone, outside of showing them unconditional love, was "to ask them about themselves and make them feel significant." So every single time you ask him one of these 237 questions and really listen to his responses, you're paying him the highest compliment of all!

68. **How do you keep the romance alive in your relationship?**

Men agree that monogamy shouldn't have to be monotonous, so how do they keep the spice in their relationships? The number one answer wasn't sexy lingerie or weekend getaways. It was surprises! One Surprise Junkie proclaims: "When my wife leaves a surprise note in my pocket or gives me tickets to a concert I've been dying to see out of the blue, I fall in love with her all over again." Can we melt now?

71. **Would you consider mutual masturbation to orgasm with your partner a night of great sex?**

Surprisingly, most guys said they *would* consider this a night of mind-blowing sex--even though there is no actual penetration. As one guy put it: "85 percent of sex is touch, and only 15 percent is penetration--and I can be satisfied with 85 percent!" Other guys said that mutual masturbation was an excellent way to find out how the other person liked to be touched. And they all said that a woman who could masturbate in front of them was irresistably fearless, confident, and sexy. Go for it!

73. **Why is it so difficult for you to talk about your sexual needs?**

Guys were in almost 100% agreement on this one: *they're afraid of what we'll think of them.* "You know, at what point am I a pervert? Where does she draw that line between adventurous, and twisted? And if I cross it, what's she gonna think?" There's also the fear of hurting our feelings if they suggest a change in technique. Sounds like a lot of insecurity on both sides. The solution is to have a big "comfort zone" for open talk. This couple has it right: "One of us will bring up some outrageous fantasy, and we'll laugh about it, especially if it's pretty out there. But then the next night the other will say, 'Hey, do you really want to try that one?' Sometimes it's 'oh, no, I was only kidding,' and other times it's *bingo* – my secret dream is about to come true."

74. If you were forced to name the one aspect of your own sexuality that you least understand, what would it be?

Men said it in a hundred different ways, but the answer was always the same: a sense of *dissatisfaction* after you get the woman you want. One guy asked, "Why is it that I always want to have the *next* girl? I'm in a great relationship, love the girl I'm with, then I get this craving for some other woman" A lot of guys blamed it on their genes. But "that was good for the caveman. It's a disaster if you act like that today!" There's hope, though. The older the man, the more likely he is to have this self-destructive tendency under control.

75. How would it make you feel if your lover could not reach orgasm during intercourse without some form of manual clitoral stimulation?

Get ready for this, girls: About a third of the guys I polled said they'd feel like they weren't doing something right if you had to have some hands-on action during sex. (Duh!) But thankfully two out of three knew the importance of manual or oral clitoral stimulation. "Since her love button is where it all happens, I spend hours touching, licking, and sucking it," said one enlightened lover. "I mean, how many guys can get off unless you do something to old Mr. Friendly?" Right on!

77. If a woman wanted to intensify your orgasm, what words should she whisper in your ear right before you climax?

Here was a surprise: over 90% complained about how *little* their lovers actually talk in bed. "Anything she said out loud would be incredible!" several guys said. But when they got down to it, two magic words came up time and time again: "I'm coming!" Or, as one *guy* put it: "I'm coming, I'm coming, *I'm coming*, Oh God, oh yes, right now, that's it, don't stop *I'm coo-ming!*" Most men see their lover's orgasm as permission to blast-off. "Until she tells me she's there, I'm doing everything I can not to come – reciting baseball stats, or the Pledge of Allegiance." Other send-him-over the edge phrases: "F*@# me!," "You're so big!" and "Come inside me!" So go ahead, ladies – say it loud and say it proud!

82. Have you ever been caught masturbating? If so, by whom?

Guess what – many of the boys out there have been caught red-handed! One explained, "My best friend walked in on me! He couldn't see what I was doing under the blanket, but for about ten minutes I laid in bed talking to him, trying to not make it obvious that I was slowly pulling my underwear back up." Talk about embarrassing. Another confessed, "Yep, it was Mom. *The worst!* She just froze for a second, then turned around and left. I never heard a single word about it." The top answer was wives or live-in girlfriends, and in many cases the encounter caused hurt feelings: "She took it as an insult, like sex with her wasn't good enough." Hey, *we* do it – why shouldn't they?

86. Who's responsible for the female orgasm?

This gave the guys a great opportunity to be a wiseass! "Black and Decker" was a popular response, as was "Thomas Edison." (Vibrator envy, perhaps?) Another joker said, "Who's responsible? God, that's who! Isn't that the name you girls call out all the time? 'Oh God Oh God, Oh God!!'" Yet another comedian replied, "Brad Pitt, I guess. That's who she's thinking about the whole time she's doing me!" What is he, a mind reader? However, the majority of guys feel that it's *our* responsibility. "If I can't get you there, draw me a roadmap and by God I'll find a way," said one Orgasm Explorer. But you've gotta be the one to tell him, ladies, 'cause we all know that guys hate asking for directions!

 **HEART QUESTIONS/ANSWERS**

27. **What sexy celebrity do you most feel women could learn from?**

I was certain the most popular answer would be Marilyn Monroe, since she's my personal favorite. But while she did get quite a few votes, the top three names were Sharon Stone, Shania Twain, and Pamela Lee Anderson. Why? *Sexual confidence* was the quality that most mesmerized these fans.

28. **Would you like your lady to pursue you sexually more often? What percent of the time would you like her to make the sexual advances?**

Every single man responded with an enthusiastic "Yes!" to the first part of this question. Without a doubt, they want to be seduced . . . but how often? Answers ranged up to 100%, but I was surprised to find that most clustered right around 30%. The vast majority of men – just about two-thirds – wanted the woman to take control 1 time out of 3.

29 **When you're in love, what's the one thing that you can't get enough of?**

Would it surprise you to find out that the number one answer was the same for both men and women? And, no, it's not sex! It's touching --expressing affection through physical contact. But holding hands barely made the top five. Way more men preferred walking with their arm around their lover or sitting on a sofa with legs entwined. And kissing was a big favorite, as was "spooning" in bed. The biggest surprise? Guys love it when we sit in their laps. So go ahead, tell Santa what you want for Christmas!

31. **Your lover has just tied your hands behind your back and wants you to tell her how to give you the ultimate hand-job. What tips and tricks do you give her? And where's the wildest place you've ever received manual stimulation?**

When it came to hands-on action, guys were happy to say what they wanted--and where they wanted it! As far as tips and tricks: "Don't be afraid to be too rough with it!" was the number-one answer. Another popular response? "Saliva. Lots of saliva." Lick those palms, ladies! As for the wildest place they've ever received a hand-hummer, responses ranged from a dark, quiet restaurant to a crowded baseball game. A fan reminisced, "We were sitting on the bleachers during an unseasonably cold baseball game, and she put a blanket on my lap and started stroking me. I went wild!" Now that's what I call a seventh inning stretch!

35 **What are the major factors in a lasting relationship?**

I *loved* these answers. There wasn't one big favorite, but the ones that came up again and again were: Trust, communication, love, honesty, laughter, security, strong values, respect and a healthy sex life. I think any woman would agree.

41. **What adult video do you think every woman should watch at least once?**

Why? Several men mentioned favorite videos with specific acts they wished their wives or girlfriends would master – some of which, I swear, look like Hollywood special effects to me. But two names came up more often than any other: *The Devil In Miss Jones*, with Georgina Spelvin, and *anything* starring Marilyn Chambers. They're both classics, shot with bigger budgets and more care than most erotic videos out today, but that's not what made them special. It's the attitude of the stars. "She's not a freak, or some nasty whore. It's just so obvious that she's just a great woman who truly enjoys hot sex." Now *there's* a role model! Both films are out on video now.

47. Jack Moran, a renowned clinical psychologist, has cooked up the following Erotic Equation: Obstacles + Attraction = Hot Sex. What's *your* erotic equation?

I hope you're not expecting serious answers here, because I sure didn't get any! Several dreamers piped up with "Two Women + Me = Hot Sex!" Uh-huh. In a sign of the times, more than a quarter of the guys tossed Viagra into the equation. But the most common answer was a variation on this: Beer + Women = Hot Sex. (Although, in my experience, Too MUCH Beer + Men = *no* sex!)

48. Which type of lingerie makes you heart race? What totally turns you off?

The top response was no surprise – but the second one sure was! Today's man likes the same thing his great-grandfather did: stockings and a garter belt, the first choice of nine out of ten. Hot on its high heels: a man's white dress shirt, with panties underneath. Easy, comfortable, affordable and sexy – what a combo! Men love teddies and silky gowns; surprisingly, they don't much care for baby dolls and other "little girl" looks. What about warm, comfy flannel? "Oh, please, she might as well be wearing a sign that says Not Tonight!"

53. What do women find sexy that most men don't? What do men find sexy that most women don't?

The guys must have had a secret meeting before I asked the first question, because they pretty much all had the same answer: Lots of makeup. Guess the Tammy Faye Baker look is officially out! Another libido-killer? Tons of perfume. "Most guys are allergic," said one sniffling stud. "Please cool it on the cologne!" On the latter part of the question, most guys said that a quickie with no foreplay was a decidedly male turn-on. Said one Quickie Fan, "If it was up to me, I'd have quick, spontaneous sex every time we did it. But women need to be tuned up and primed for passion!" You got that right, buddy!

54. What sexual insecurities do you have?

Even though they may not act like it, men are just as insecure about their bodies and lovemaking techniques as we are. In fact, almost every man I talked to felt inadequate one way or the other. One guy said: "I'm embarrassed to say this since I'm 37 years old, but my main insecurity is, *'Am I doing this right?'*" Other guys were insecure about their love handles or ejaculating too soon. And, of course, several brought up the classic male concern: not being big enough. *Repeat after me, guys. It's not the size of the wand– it's the magic in it!*

58. If you could receive a surprise package right before sex, what would be in it?

What did *your* guy say to this one? The answers I received ran from sexy to sweet to just plain bizarre. Men asked for: massage oil, candles, condoms, marijuana, a six-pack, a winning lottery ticket, Godiva chocolates, breath mints, and an actual woman. Maybe it's only because it's been in the news so much, but the most popular answer was *Viagra*. "Think of it as our version of the Wonderbra," cracked one guy. "It just makes us a little better than we really are!"

15. **If you were to pick the one alluring quality that draws you to a woman and keeps you there, what would it be?**

Just when you think you have men figured out, they throw you a real surprise. They love a lot of things about us, but their favorite quality had nothing to do with sex--at least, not directly. "It's that willingness to laugh, a sense of humor," said most of the men I interviewed. "Because if you can't laugh together, you can't live together." Remember what men said to, What makes a woman unforgettable? It was her smile.

16. **What makes a lady a *lady* – and what makes her look like anything but?**

Wow – what a variety of answers I got on this one. Most guys said they couldn't quite describe what makes a lady a lady, but they know it when they see it. One man said, "It's the way she walks, the way she talks, the way she communicates with you, her vocabulary, everything." But when it came to the sort of woman they would not like to commit to, guys got way more specific. The three big turn-offs were: Women who use foul language (except in bed), women who flirt shamelessly with other guys, and women who try too hard.

19. **What type of woman turns you off emotionally and sexually?**

Is there a difference? Who says guys like dumb blondes? Apparently, they don't like dumb blondes, brunettes, or redheads--because "Stupid women" was overwhelmingly the number-one answer. And when it came to emotional and sexual turn-offs, most guys said they were one in the same. "I can't be sexually turned on by someone who doesn't turn me on intellectually," said one sage soul. "If there's no emotional connection, I'm not interested." So I guess boys do want us for our brains as well as our bodies! Yippee!

20. **When does a woman's body look the most beautiful to you?**

"When she's naked!" was the most obvious answer I got. But when pressed for details, guys got more specific. Runners-up: "Right out of the shower, still wet." "Bent over, with that beautiful bottom in the air." "In front of the fireplace, stretched out on pillows." My personal favorite? "When she's pregnant with my baby." Sweet! Ah, but one was the clear favorite of more than 60% of these guys: they're wild about a *woman on top*.

21. **What do you think about when you touch a woman's inner thigh?**

This answer prompted the sexiest and sweetest responses. Some obviously said they're thinking about getting laid. But surprisingly the most popular answer I received was: "What do I think about? The gates of heaven." As one guy put it: "You're thinking about opening those gates. You spend all your time trying to get there and when she finally leans back and parts her knees, you're looking on the Holy of Holies, the Sanctum Sanctorum. It's heaven's gate." Seriously sexy!

24. **If a woman had to wear the same clothes for an entire week – frequently washed, of course! – what would you like to see her wear?**

This one sure isn't what you expect! I wasn't too surprised when some men wanted sexy lingerie or the cheerleader uniform, but I could hardly believe it when this answer became the clear favorite: Jeans and a T-shirt! Why? One guy summed it up perfectly when he said: "There's nothing more attractive than a woman who's really comfortable."